A Lens Into
Executive Retirement
from the Spouse/Partner
Perspective

DEBBIE DELLINGER
MyNextSeason

Library of Congress Cataloging-in-Publication Data
Dellinger, Debbie
Living Into Your Next Season: Moving Forward After the Crisis of 2020
ISBN- 979-8-669-17848-2

Cover and Book Design: Scattaregia Design
First edition published 2020 by MyNextSeason Printed in the United States of America

DEDICATION

....

This book is dedicated to **Frances Fetterolf**, who influenced many with her seismic energy to create justice where there was none. Had she been born into a later generation, she would have been CEO of a major company. As it was, she captured our attention and our hearts.

TABLE OF CONTENTS

PREFACE

MyNextSeason was founded in 2014 with a vision of providing comprehensive executive transition support that included an optional "spouse session." Little did we know it would become one of the most wanted, feared, sensitive, hopeful, and anxiety-producing parts of our process!

We quickly found the "spouse session" had a lot of emotion tied to it—both for the participating executive and for their spouse/partner. After all, most things in life that really matter are emotionally charged—and how the marriage is going to work post-retirement-transition is one such thing.

Perhaps with the "spouse conversation" we are treading on sacred space: a door with a padlock to which only two people have the key. Or, perhaps we are entering a room that has simply lain dormant, dark, or unoccupied for some time. Regardless, retirement transitions seem to stir the spirit and taunt the soul! They awaken frustrations and marital rifts—buried beneath the non-optional, intrusive-to-the-family demands that successful careers are built on. They also contain the most optimistic, hopeful, prayerful possibilities that both members cling to, even in the absence of conversation or comparison of notes.

No one *really* likes the effect of the corporate lifestyle on marriage/ spouse/partner relationships—but everyone gets used to it and adapts life patterns accordingly. Balance and joy are reached and found—but with retirement, all of that suddenly shifts . . . and no one knows what the new rules are.

Retirement transitions shine floodlights on marriage health with nowhere to hide. And with that exposure comes the opportunity to communicate, share, explore together, and walk out with a clear plan about the future. Done well, it can be magical and healing. Done poorly, it can widen the divide and add fuel to burning embers.

Because importance meets fragility when it comes to the spouse/partner point-of-view on retirement transitions, we wanted to pause and draw attention to the topic—with the greatest respect we could possibly muster. We wanted to hear the voices of those who had lived through the transition (or were living through it) and get their advice for others. We wanted to hear from them—what made the transition easier or less easy—and what success looked like to them. That's how this study, *The Retiring Spouse/Partner Project,* was born.

Deborah Dellinger, MyNextSeason's Director of External Engagement, who has consulted with hundreds of executives in transition, had herself lived through such a transition with her executive spouse. So, along with her professional experience, she brought personal sensitivity.

The responses were thoughtful, introspective, vulnerable, helpful, and raw. Debbie treaded carefully into that sacred space and came out with great wisdom to share with future spouse/partners as they anticipate and prepare for retirement transitions of their own—or their spouse/partner's. Highlights included:

- Communicate with your retiring executive authentically and early in the process

- Establish boundaries for your life, your goals, and your physical space

- Maintain separate offices—this was almost universally shared as a best practice

- Decide what activities you will do solo, and what you will do as a couple.

The conclusions presented here are profound, helpful, and easy to apply. This is one of those areas where we can be better—and where we *need* to be better. The findings of this book are important for all of us to understand.

Thank you, Debbie, for having the courage to walk through that padlocked door and emerge with insights that will be helpful to all couples who are preparing to/navigating retirement transitions. Thank you to the spouse/partners whose trust you earned, who chose to share their experiences—painful and uplifting, humorous and hopeful, insightful and calming.

We are all better for the sharing of words between the covers of this book.

Leslie W. Braksick, PhD, MPH
Co-Founder and Senior Partner
MyNextSeason

The Retiring Spouse/Partner Project

R etirement is a major life transition, affecting not only the retiree, but the family—and specifically the spouse, partner, or significant other. Different from prior generations, current executives upon retirement may have decades of runway with which to carve out a first "next season" with their loved ones—and many next seasons beyond that.

Approached with intention and discernment, this transition from an all-in, all-encompassing, all-engaging career can position both the executive and spouse/partner for new and exciting possibilities personally, relationally, and vocationally. MYNEXTSEASON has supported hundreds of retiring clients and their spouse/partners in this journey, and we have learned that sharing the experiences of those who have gone before—the voices of those that have "been there and done that"—is invaluable for those facing the experience of having a loved one retire.

The book is designed to—

- Support you in preparation for this important next season.

- Serve as a basis for conversation with your spouse/partner and family.

- Provide the ability to anticipate the joys and pitfalls others have experienced.

- Enable you to "look around the corner" through the lens of others, who like you, want this transition to happen well.

We asked some special people to share their personal journey—specifically, the spouses and partners of those in our MYNEXTSEASON network of family, friends, and clients who have experienced retirement. Every retirement is unique, brought about by a variety of circumstances, not always sought or welcomed. Those who agreed to share their experiences come from a variety of backgrounds. While some retirements were anticipated well ahead by virtue of mandatory retirement ages or known succession plans, others were sudden and not by choice.

Everyone interviewed gifted this project with their time as well as thoughtful, honest answers. Their responses are presented anonymously to ensure that each felt comfortable answering our questions with candor and veracity. We have provided a bio for each spouse/partner who participated. We are thankful for the wisdom and perspective they offered, without which we would not have this book to support you

The Process

We provided each participant with interview questions relating to their experiences as their spouse/partner retired, to prepare them for an interview with Debbie Dellinger, Director of External Engagement. The interview questions were:

1. Who determined the timing of your spouse/partner's transition?

2. How is the transition going for you? In what ways have you felt supported?

3. What is/was your role as spouse/partner? Is it changing?

4. Do you have time to dream about the things you want to do post-transition?

5. In hindsight, is there anything that could have made that transition more successful (or perhaps less painful)?

6. What advice would you have to spouse/partners of other executives who are preparing for this major transition?

7. What are you happy to leave behind? How is your spouse/partner handling the transition?

MyNextSeason has a cadre of Advisors, all former executives who have transitioned well and now work 1:1 with our retiring executive clients as part of our retirement transition methodology. These Advisors have collectively worked with hundreds of the most senior leaders to support their retirement transitions.

We feel that it is important for you to hear their voices pertaining to the spouse/partner experience of retirement. We asked them to respond to these three questions:

1. What issues are most often discussed regarding spouse/partners or between spouse/partners?

2. What issues are not being discussed, but should be? (what is the elephant in the room that everyone is ignoring?)

3. Is there anything we can do to help these discussions with your clients?

WHAT WE FOUND

After years of autonomy and self-sufficiency, your executive is retiring from a hard-charging, intense career. Transitions are hard, made harder because this one involves you, your executive, and your expectations, including dreams put off during the hectic pace and stress of working, traveling, and building a life together.

Done well, transitioning from a main career offers the opportunity to pause and become intentional in discerning the possibilities for this next season, separately and together. We found six common themes in the stories, hopes, and experiences of the twenty-six spouse/partners interviewed for this book. These six themes, detailed in Chapter 2, comprise key areas to consider and explore as you anticipate and embark on this next season:

1. Prepare for a range of emotions
2. Retain your identity
3. Communicate authentically
4. Rekindle your relationship and attend to your health
5. Prioritize family and friends
6. Enjoy the new season

It is our hope that, armed with the voices of those who have undertaken this journey, yours will lead to a season of purpose and fulfillment. Just as you and your significant other made adjustments to eventually learn how to live and create a life together, the experiences related in this book will begin to familiarize you with the landscape of your new circumstances so that you can navigate this journey well and discover what's next.

1. Prepare for a Range of Emotions

You and your executive partner have earned the right to choose what you want to do next—individually and together. Yet the uncertainty of changing from a life you know to one that you determine can elicit myriad emotions. The spouse/partners in our study shared feelings of fear, relief, excitement, and shock. Some were surprised by the uncertainty they saw in their executive—a trait they were not used to experiencing with their decisive, hard-charging mate. Some wondered what changes retirement would bring, including a move or downsizing. Moreover, the spouse/partner wondered if they were really ready for their executive to retire and what that could entail.

2. Retain Your Identity

Every person interviewed expressed that they were not "retiring" from the lives and the work they created while their executive pursued their career. Joint planning was cited as critical to the spouse/partner so there would be time allotted for shared activities or projects. However—and without exception—setting boundaries around offices and kitchen duties were a major part of the adjustment to retirement. Additionally, while some felt the need to delay their own retirement to allow their executive the space and time to acclimate to retirement and "figure things out," all worked on learning how to coordinate calendars and integrate the retiring executive into the family and household.

3. Communicate Authentically

The key to a smooth transition and harmonious regrouping of relationship, family, and friends is communicating well. Many in the study group shared they felt their executive's retirement impacted them and other members of the family as much as it did the executive. Dependent on the communication style inherent in the relationship, most participants reported sharing expectations about individual needs and sharing life together. Dreaming together about what life could be like was exciting. Many took this time to pause together and discuss ideas, both long-held and new, for a renewed partnership and relationship.

4. Rekindle Your Relationship and Attend to Your Health

Overwhelmingly, the study group enjoyed the benefit of their executive unwinding and reconnecting. The demands of their careers, including long hours and travel, had made for little time to relax and experience a cadence of life that allowed for simple pleasures; all retired exhausted. Some participants rediscovered the person they fell in love with and truly appreciated the opportunity to be together without the ubiquity of an intense career. Others shared that their retiring executive prioritized their relationship and their needs in a novel way. Health was an issue for some retiring couples in that it predicated their next season; for others it became a touchpoint for gratitude.

5. Prioritize Family and Friends

Both the retiring executive and spouse/partner welcomed the opportunity to spend more time with children, grandchildren, and extended family. Participants reported how wonderful it was to spend time with children and family as a couple and share parental and grandparenting responsibilities. Friends took on another dimension. Some relationships did not withstand the transition to retirement, while others were renewed. New relationships developed as interests and activities were explored. For some, faith coalesced family and friends and offered meaningful commitments to community.

6. Enjoy the New Season

The study group continued to emphasize the need for communication—sharing your perspective and listening in equal measure. Many wished they would have started conversations about expectations earlier—before retirement became a reality. Laying track for activities and interests early was important to those who did so; others felt, in retrospect, they should have explored them sooner.

Many reported wonder in discovering their executive anew, coupled with connecting over shared purposes and supporting individual pursuits. Participants learned to accept and expect adjustments and changes as each became situated and comfortable in this first next season. Finally, there was gratitude for their experiences, their executive mate, and the life they are sharing.

CHAPTER ONE

Those Who Participated

The lens through which we experience twenty-six unique retirements is provided by their spouse/ partners: twenty-five women and one man. It is their voice, their journey, and their viewpoint, spoken to you, the reader, in anticipating choices you may make as your executive retires.

The industries represented by the executives of this study group include banking, insurance, oil and gas, manufacturing, healthcare, transportation, higher education, telecommunications, and private equity.

Seven of our participants were working fulltime as professionals, business owners, entrepreneurs, and executives in publicly traded companies at the time of their executive partner's retirement. At the time each was interviewed, some had experienced the retirement transition ten years prior, while others were newly retired. Some chose to continue working when their loved one retired, while others had left the workforce at various times to raise a family, to relocate, and/or to meet the demands of their executive's career.

In 2017, MyNextSeason, under the direction of Project Leader Valerie Johnson, completed a book entitled *Reflections on the Journey from Executive Spouses*. It captured the voices of those preparing for the role of C-suite executive spouse/partner and all that entails. Twenty-five people participated in that project, and of those, five had experienced retirement with their executive. Valerie asked those five spouse/partners the seven questions above, and their responses, related with candor and care, are represented in the data put forth in the ensuing pages.

Twenty-six people comprise our study group, and all are actively pursuing a variety of interesting activities and work, as you will discover when you read their bios.

BIOS

Jan Berardi

Married 50 years and with nine grandchildren, Jan Berardi has been a steady force in the lives of her husband and family. With humor, warmth, and strength, she and Frank raised three children, including a set of twins, while relocating around the country to support his career as a senior executive with Allstate. Jan has transitioned several times. As Frank moved from corporate life, he founded an executive coaching firm, Callahan, where he supported hundreds of executives, became an executive coach at CLG, and now is an Advisor with MYNEXTSEASON.

Jan retired as a registered nurse after working part-time for years in both intensive care and obstetrics/gynecology. After attending nursing school at St. Vincent's in Jacksonville, Florida, she met Frank while working at the University of Florida hospital, where he was a student. Jan is known to create delicious Italian food, true to her heritage. She is in a book club, Bible study, and enjoys playing golf with Frank. They maintain homes in Chicago and Florida, where they host family and friends throughout the year. Originally from central Florida, Jan has enjoyed all the Midwest offers. She and Frank play active roles in the Main Street Organization, a not-for-profit that supports business leaders to transform main streets into charming environments where businesses can thrive.

Carol Braksick

Carol Braksick enjoyed parenting three wonderful children while her husband, Norm, pursued a career with The Upjohn Company as V.P. in Agriculture Marketing and then President of The Asgrow Seed Company. After his retirement, he served as Volunteer Executive Director of a nonprofit organization for five years. Carol found fulfillment in volunteer activities such as Hospice, but her most rewarding adventure was guiding a refugee family from Rwanda through acclimating to life in the U.S., citizenship, and education. Her grandchildren and great-grandchild bring her joy upon joy, gifts that only other grandparents can understand.

Norm's career, involving extensive travel, led to parallel lives, which resulted in a retirement that surprised them by their lack of preparedness. Loving each other deeply was not sufficient to smoothly traverse a new path. They had always heard "You can't live on love," and now they were experiencing it! A good sense of humor and doing their best to accommodate each other helped, but there was still a sense of frustration. The advice she gives and wishes she had when they needed it: Get help wherever you can find it!

Judy Brust

Judy Brust is an accomplished artist who, at the age of fifty, followed her dreams and earned a Masters in Fine Arts from SUNY, Albany. She holds a bachelor's degree in art education from Penn State University. A strong advocate for pursuing your own interests while actively supporting a spouse's executive career, Judy began selling her sculptures and paintings at art shows while at home raising children full time.

Judy attributes fifty years of teamwork with her husband as the key to successfully managing careers, raising their three children, and enjoying retirement. Bob Brust retired from General Electric as VP, Finance after 32 years of service. He then became CFO at Unisys, then Kodak, then Sprint, working twelve more years and leaving the workforce for good in 2011. Bob and Judy have eight grandchildren and split time between homes in Captiva, FL and Nantucket, MA. Judy maintains art studios in both locations and continues to find joy in producing and showing her work. She also enjoys spending time with her growing family.

Gail Canizares

The parents of five children and grandparents to nine, Gail Canizares is as serious an introvert as her husband Rob is an extrovert. Through two career transitions, Gail and Rob lived internationally in Amsterdam, Hong Kong, France, and Brazil. Gail met Rob as a freshman in a French class at Cornell. She earned her Education degree at Vanderbilt University and a Master's in Middle School Education at the University of Wisconsin, Lacrosse. Gail has taught at every level from Montessori preschool to college. She especially loved teaching at a middle school and small Catholic school, Viterbo University in Wisconsin. She used her Master's thesis to improve the foreign language program in the elementary, middle, and high schools in Onalaska, WI. Gail is active with The Innocence Project, whose mission is to free the wrongfully convicted and incarcerated and reform the system responsible for their unjust imprisonment.

Rob spent most of his career with American Standard, retiring in 2001, and took a year-long sabbatical during which he discovered that Pittsburgh is among the best places to retire. Setting aside that idea as ridiculous, he was ironically offered the presidency at Mine Safety Appliance company (MSA Safety) a year later, headquartered in Pittsburgh! He accepted, and Gail and Rob discovered Pittsburgh is a great place to live. They have continued to reside there since his MSA retirement in 2011.

Bette Cruikshank

With great passion and energy, Bette Cruikshank advocates pursuing what you love. Through multiple moves, her husband's tech industry career, and early retirement, Bette learned to embrace change and find new ways to make a difference. She holds a University of Michigan pharmaceutical degree and practiced pharmacy for eleven years prior to staying home full-time to raise two children, now grown. Bette is married to Kirk Cruikshank, former President and CEO of startup Trading Dynamics, which sold in 2000. When the children were young and Kirk was building his career, Bette threw herself into their school, fundraising to enhance the arts and music program and teaching music as a volunteer for five years. She also was a long-term PTA member and President.

For the past ten years, Bette has been active in Summit League, a not-for-profit fundraiser to support charitable organizations throughout the Silicon Valley. She is an avid reader, watercolor artist, and enjoys physical activity at their home in Los Gatos, CA and summers on Lake Sunapee, NH. Recently, her son and his wife moved to the Bay Area with their two sons, now ages 3 and 1. Her daughter also returned to the Bay Area as a Nurse Practitioner and Midwife in San Francisco. Bette and Kirk love having family nearby.

Cathy Dean

Cathy Dean has a zest for life, family, and friends, visible in the Facebook postings of her Happy Feet around the country, doing what she loves best: enjoying people and places. Originally from Flagstaff, Cathy and Vince met at the University of Arizona as students. As parents of two grown children, Cathy was supportive of Vince as he transitioned from an early corporate career in development/construction of retirement communities with numerous relocations, to co-founding Dean Development Inc., specializing in commercial construction, management, and real estate development in the Kansas City area.

Cathy has been part of the Junior League and loved supporting her children's schools. She found she loved library work and volunteered at the high school library in Prairie Village, KS for 20 years, retiring 3 years ago. Her passion for needlecrafts always has her working on a project or two. Her creativity extends to knitting and jewelry-making. On any given weekend in spring, summer, and fall, Cathy and Vince can be found at a racetrack around the country where Vince races vintage cars or at their Lake of the Ozarks home. Cathy loves to rest her Happy Feet at home in Leawood, KS with Vince and their cocker spaniel, Trixie Lou Snickerdoodle.

Bonnie Downen

Bonnie Downen exudes Texan hospitality and a can-do attitude in both her family and work life. A musician at heart, Bonnie recently retired from teaching music at a private preschool in Charlotte, NC. She is married to Dick, who retired as Chief Administrative Executive of Wealth Management for Bank of America. Bonnie has been active raising their three children, teaching Sunday school, and volunteering at their schools, including being a room parent for 18 years.

An advocate for children and education, Bonnie earned a teaching degree from Sam Houston State University and taught kindergarten for 10 years. She has been active in the Junior League in Plano, TX and Charlotte, volunteering as a reading tutor and mentor to students in the public schools. She started a Mothers of Young Children group in Texas and taught a course about the importance of children reporting abuse of any kind to someone in authority. She has been an avid supporter of St. Jude Children's Research Hospital for many years and chaired the annual Charlotte Showhouse and Auction fundraiser, receiving special recognition in 2009 for her leadership. Bonnie and Dick are new grandparents and reside in Charlotte.

Fran Fetterolf

Fran Fetterolf was "a woman who got things done." Recognized as a leader in college, she was Pan-Hellenic President and elected to "Who's Who" for college students in America. Fran met future husband Fred at Grove City College, and they raised two children while relocating countrywide as Fred worked his way up to become Alcoa's COO. Upon settling in Sewickley, PA, she became the part-time Executive Assistant to the President of the Pittsburgh Leadership Foundation.

Fran was especially talented in bringing people together to make a difference. Her family and friends call her the embodiment of faith and action, deeply committed to her community as a Board member of Child Health Association of Sewickley, Greater Pittsburgh Campfire, and Children's Museum of Pittsburgh. She organized the first benefit galas for Saltworks Theater Company, Communities and Schools, Tumaini Academy (a Christian school in northern Kenya), Women of Pittsburgh 2000, and Imani Christian Academy. She took special pride in her nearly 25 years with Saltworks nonprofit as Board Member, Board Chair, and Board Emeritus, instrumental in the organization's success. Fran opened her home to other community groups, including a Christmas party for homeless veterans served by Shepherd's Heart. She was generous and candid in her August 2016 interview, and sadly passed away in April 2017 at the age of 86.

Sherry Forsee

With great compassion for improving the lives of others, Sherry Forsee lives a life of service to her family and community. Now retired and with two daughters living close by in Kansas City, KS, Sherry and her husband, Gary, enjoy being with their six grandchildren. With 30 years of experience in telecommunications, Gary is the former CEO of Sprint. He also served as President of the University of Missouri System for three years prior to retiring in 2011.

Sherry sat on the board of Loose Foundation, which grants funds to organizations that offer social services for needy children and families in the greater Kansas City area. Currently, Sherry is active with Wayside Waifs Animal Shelter and helped create Purr Gamma Bark, a sorority of women that fosters awareness and provides financial support for the shelter. She continues to support the Rose Brooks Domestic Violence Center following time on its board. The first of her family to go to college, Sherry holds a teaching degree from Southeast Missouri State.

Phil Gulley

An educator and advocate for underserved at-risk populations, Phil Gulley praises his 48-year partnership with wife Joan in managing their opportunities and careers well. When Joan was PNC Financial Services Group's CHRO in Pittsburgh, Phil pursued a long-held passion—working with kids—volunteering for 14 years as a teacher's aide in a therapeutic preschool classroom Family Resources child abuse prevention and treatment program. He was an active board member for Staunton Farm Foundation, LEAD Pittsburgh, and Carnegie Museum of Natural History. A stay-at-home parent for their infant son while Joan was COO of The Massachusetts Company of Boston, Phil also ran corporate training/development for Bolt Beranek & Newman, a Cambridge high-tech. He directed education/consulting services for a consortium of high-techs and MIT's Sloan School to study quality management, growing to almost 100 companies and 20 universities.

While she worked at the Federal Reserve in DC, Phil worked at Georgetown and Catholic Universities. He also was Dean of Students at St. Mary's College of Maryland. His degrees are in English (Trinity College, Hartford, CT), counseling and student personnel administration (M.Ed., University of Rochester), and higher education administration (Ph.D., Boston College). He and Joan retired to Nantucket and Vero Beach, FL and love golf, bridge, reading, travel, and hiking.

Linda Higdon

Linda Higdon is an award-winning documentary filmmaker, global champion for women, and founder of Global Heart Journeys. She combines her 16 years of experience in philanthropic activism into a one-of-a-kind African luxury excursion into the hidden treasures of Kenya. Travelers gain exclusive access to women igniting change in the developing world. They meet a Nobel Peace Prize nominee, enter a global showcase for girls' education, and secluded villages and tribal communities, expanding the mind and heart and enriching the senses.

Linda's husband, Paul Higdon, recently retired as Dean of Global Credit Training for Bank of America. For the past 3 years, while partnering with Linda's endeavors in Kenya, he published his first book, *Hope and a Future: Life, Survival and Renewal on the Streets of an African Slum.* Growing from nearly 20 years of philanthropic work in Kenya, it chronicles the true story of a street boy, John Maina, who, in a Kenyan sense, is his son. Linda is a creative for all times. During COVID-19 she is raising funds for emergency food relief for the rural starvation-trapped Kenyan children and their families she loves. When not traveling to remote areas of the world, Paul and Linda live near Lake Geneva, Wisconsin.

Debi Justice

Growing up in a military family gave Debi Justice a unique ability to accept change and embrace the opportunities she would encounter as an executive's spouse. She met her husband Rick while working at Hewlett-Packard (HP) in sales support, and became a full-time at-home parent and active volunteer when their children were young. Rick Justice worked for HP for 22 years prior to joining Cisco Systems in 1996. He retired in 2009 as Cisco's EVP of Worldwide Operations and Business Development.

Debi cites their time as a young family in Hong Kong as transformative to how she views the world. While overseas, she engaged in the American Women's Association and relied on a strong support network of ex-pat spouses. Back in the U.S., Debi's volunteer focus turned to education, serving on various school/university boards and committees. Most recently she has helped Cancer Care Point, which provides counseling, nutrition, yoga, and caregiver support at no charge. She enjoys traveling with Rick and spending time with their three children and six grandchildren. They live in northern California and enjoy considerable time in Hawaii.

Laureen Kernan

 Family time is important to Laureen Kernan. She spent summers on her grandparents' dairy farm, learning the close bond of family and importance of a solid work ethic. Married to Jay Kernan, retired Managing Partner of PricewaterhouseCoopers' Minneapolis office since 1986, Laureen pursues her interests while supporting her husband's. First of her family in college, she graduated from Chicago's Loyola University and joined PwC's audit practice for 5 years. She transitioned to accounting and finance at Kraft General Foods and Philip Morris for 5 more years and left to tend her active, growing family.

Together, Laureen and Jay have six children 25–43 and five grandchildren. (The elder three are "bonus kids" from Jay's first marriage.) The tight-knit family is spread from LA to NY, with family vacations shared in Italy, Ireland, France, New York, Chicago, Napa Valley, and Utah's national parks. Jay and Laureen are deeply involved with Folds of Honor, a not-for-profit supporting education of families of killed/disabled veterans. Laureen loves to work out, cook, hike, read, play golf, and Mahjong. She credits the joy in her marriage to their supportive relationship, and loving/liking each other throughout their marriage, rediscovering their compatibility upon his retirement. They love Arizona life with golf, hiking, enjoying friends, and watching the mountains change color.

Becky Linsz

Armed with a degree in economics from Wheaton College, Becky Linsz has been an advocate for the underserved her entire life. She worked for World Relief early in her career as a Regional Representative, concentrating on international economic development and fundraising. Throughout many corporate moves, and as full-time parent to three daughters, Becky has volunteered with Opportunity International, helping them launch international initiatives in the financial products offered including education financing.

Married to Mark Linsz, former Treasurer of Bank of America and now Co-Founder and Senior Managing Partner of MyNextSeason, Becky has lived in Hong Kong, London, and various locations in the U.S. Originally from Huntsville, Alabama, Becky enjoys international travel, volunteering with Freedom Communities in Charlotte, NC; musical theater; and designing jewelry. Becky and Mark relish mentoring young people and open their home in Charlotte to a variety of groups, including those from The Charlotte Fellows and their church.

Julie Markham

Julie Cannon Markham has spent her life learning and trying new experiences. As a young mother, she taught oil painting techniques at a community college. She learned to play organ for her LDS congregation in New Jersey, a life-long passion that included accompanying several *Messiah* performances. She discovered the joy of family history research and publishes family histories online; when others find them, they often make these works collaborative. Her shelves are lined with world history books she is making time to read.

Married to Ben S. Markham, retired chemical engineer and VP of Engineering at ExxonMobil Research and Engineering, Julie spent much of her life relocating and raising children along the way. As active members of The Church of Jesus Christ of Latter-day Saints, making friends in new places became easy. Ben currently is a branch president of a hundred-strong LDS congregation in an assisted living center, where Julie teaches Sunday School and often accompanies the residents' choir. She recently enjoyed her fifteen minutes of fame after photographing the transformation of a tragically burned pioneer tabernacle into an LDS temple. Blog readers worldwide followed her pictures, often teaching her what her camera saw. Ben and Julie have five children and many grandchildren, doing their best to get the latter into as much trouble as possible.

Catharine Ryan

Catharine Murray Ryan was born in Bronxville, NY. Graduating from New Rochelle's Ursuline School, she attended Newton College of the Sacred heart, earning her BA in Economics *cum laude* in 1968, and Master's in Pastoral Ministry from Duquesne University in 1993. Catharine and her husband John, retired Chairman and CEO of Mine Safety Appliance Company (MSA Safety), have lived in Pittsburgh since 1969. While raising their three children, Catharine served as a Chaplain at Magee Women's Hospital and Forbes Regional Hospital, a Trustee of Children's Hospital of Pittsburgh of UPMC for 13 years, and Board Member of the Children's Hospital of Pittsburgh Foundation for 7 years, the last 3 as Chair.

In 2002, she and Fr. Drew Morgan, C.O., co-founded the National Institute for Newman Studies (NINS), launching *Newman Studies Journal*, developing the Newman library collection, hosting 70+ Newman scholars worldwide, and raising funds for the Gailliot Center for Newman Studies. Currently, she is on Duquesne University's

Board and is a retired Trustee and Fellow of The Catholic University of America. Seton Hill University awarded her the Elizabeth Ann Seton Medal in 2012. She spends summers on Cape Cod with family, including four grandsons, enjoying gardening, sailing, biking, and reading. In Pittsburgh, she enjoys the Pittsburgh Ballet Theatre, Pittsburgh Symphony Orchestra, and fine art museums.

Carolyn Sabatini

Carolyn Sabatini retired from Pharmavite after 29 years in 2019 as the Vice President of Government Relations and Chair of the Pharmavite PAC. Carolyn worked on both coasts while living in Leawood, Kansas with her husband Ken. Whether meeting with elected Congressional officials and their staff in Washington, the corporate staff in California, or national health professional organizations, Carolyn brought a rare combination of pragmatism and enthusiasm to her work. She created a successful career spanning 35+ years in product management, new product development, national account sales, and stints at both Con Agra and Unilever, including working in Durban, South Africa. She received a prestigious industry award in 2007 for her legislative leadership contributions from the Council for Responsible Nutrition. She also received the Pharmavite CEO Recognition award in 2005.

Carolyn has been married for 32 years to Ken, retired Senior Creative Photographer at Hallmark Cards Company and now a freelance photographer. They have two children, 30 and 28. Now retired full-time, she enjoys visiting with her adult children, entertaining friends, cooking Italian food, and traveling internationally. Carolyn graduated with Honors from California State University, Fullerton with a BA in American Studies and earned an MBA from the Peter F. Drucker School of Management at Claremont Graduate University.

Teresa Sharp

A lifelong resident of North Carolina, Teresa Sharp's life is as interesting and varied as the landscape of her native state. Teresa met her husband, Mike, at Davidson College, where she was a member of Phi Beta Kappa and graduated *magna cum laude,* with a degree in Economics. Teresa enjoyed a successful career in sales with Xerox, Sprint, and MCI until she became a full-time mother to their two sons. She is actively involved at Lake Forest Church, serving as ordained elder and part of the church "planting commission," overseeing the mission of planting churches locally and globally.

Teresa has traveled extensively to seek opportunities to grow the Church through mission trips to Kenya, Zambia, Southern Sudan, Nicaragua, and most recently Egypt. She currently leads a woman's Bible study and co-leads a weekly couple's study with Mike. She founded a Christian yoga business, aptly named YoGod, teaching people of all ages and experience. She loves to scuba dive and play pickleball with her family. She and Mike, who recently retired from Bank of America as a Senior Vice President—Project Director of Technology and Operations Group, enjoy working their organic gardens at their home on Lake Norman, NC.

Nan Smith

Nan Smith met the love of her life at Emporia State University. They married in 1985 and have two grown children, Emma and Josh. They are joyful grandparents to their granddaughter, Ruth. Nan is a woman of faith, depending on the power of prayer to guide her life's decisions. Doug and Nan have spent their lives in Kansas City. Doug was the CEO of BE Smith, a healthcare recruitment firm. They sold the business in 2016 and Doug retired. Soon after that, Doug and Nan provided the lead gift to develop and construct the *BE Smith Family Center* on the campus of Advent Health Shawnee Mission. The

Center opened in April 2019, and houses the Lee Ann Britain Infant Development Center and the Early Learning Center for Advent Health employees.

Nan was an elementary school teacher in the Shawnee Mission School District for 15 years. After leaving teaching, she became more involved in her church. Over the years, Nan has worked extensively in Women's Ministry, Congregational Care Ministry, and Crossroads Ministry. She and Doug are currently enjoying watching their children forge their lifepaths, loving being grandparents, and looking forward to getting back to the Colorado mountains very soon!

Liz Sutherlin

 Liz holds a BS in Pharmacy from the University of Sciences in Philadelphia and is a licensed pharmacist in Kansas and Pennsylvania. She spent 25 years in pharmaceutical sales, first with Merck & Co., working up to Regional Business Group VP, and then for Enturia/Cardinal Health as VP of Sales. With a passion for service, Liz was Acting Executive Director and Board President of HappyBottoms, which provides diapers to Kansas City low-income families. In late 2015, after fundraising and transitioning HappyBottoms to paid staff, Liz left as Executive Director and was named to the National Diaper Bank Network board. She also co-chaired the American Cancer Society's Shave to Save fundraisers. Liz then started her own consultancy in strategic planning and management coaching in 2018, and contracts with iBosswell, helping clients align business strategy with organizational culture.

Liz serves on the Board of Pharmacy of Grace, a non-profit providing pharmaceutical care to low-income patients in Wyandotte County, KS. She loves CrossFit training, which keeps her connected to young people, and golf. She was a Board Member of Executive Women's Golf Association, KC Metro Chapter. Liz is married to Steve Sutherlin, recently retired owner and President of Sutherlin Optical. They reside in Overland Park, KS with a blended family of four children and four grandchildren.

Tris Thorne

Believing in faith, family, and friends has been important to Tris Thorne, married to Bud for almost 51 years. Tris enjoys family and having Bud retired from a family business that kept him on the road much of the time as the lead salesperson for Consolidated Product Systems. Becoming a member of Friends of the Library led her and a dear friend to found a book club, Book Lovers Never Sleep Alone. After earning a BA in Economics from Chatham University in Pittsburgh, Tris raised her family and became a partner and Advertising Manager for *Sewickley Magazine*. She and the magazine's editor then started a successful business called Partners in Print, filling a market niche for small- and medium-sized companies. With grown children, she and her husband enjoy friendships old and new, being more involved in their church, and doing their own thing, but always connected in love and faith.

Karen Vachon

With a fourteen-year career at General Electric prior to staying home to raise children, Karen Vachon's corporate experience played a large role in shaping her understanding of the demands on her husband, Mark Vachon, the retired CEO of GE Healthcare Americas. Through many domestic and overseas moves, she has garnered wisdom on the benefits of engaging in each community and finding something she loves to do in addition to her roles as at-home mother and CEO spouse. Karen and Mark currently live in Boston, MA and are the parents of two grown children. She serves on the boards of buildOn—Boston and Project Sunapee (New Hampshire) and works weekly at The Women's Lunch Place, a day shelter in Boston. She enjoys running, biking, and skiing. Karen holds a degree in finance and international business from Siena College.

Julie Wellner

As sole owner of Wellner Architects, Julie Wellner is the consummate project manager. Whether managing the design for projects, organizing the Juvenile Diabetes Gala, or planning a family trip to Southeast Asia, Julie is detailed, calm, and professional. Graduating from the University of Kansas with three degrees (architecture, architectural engineering, environmental design), she worked for a Kansas City architectural firm. In her late 20s, she established her own firm and she has never looked back. Julie has won numerous awards for her firm's excellence in architecture, but is best known for her work at both Kansas City airports and Kansas City's new Regional Crime Lab.

Julie currently is giving back, serving on the Planned Parenthood Great Plains Board. She is married to Dennis, also an architect, who founded the firm Populous, with primary focus on designing stadium facilities for NFL teams. He and Julie are committed to community, having supported JDRF, The Hope Center, Girls to Women, and various professional architectural organizations. They have two grown children and are ardent Jayhawk, Chiefs, and Royals fans. Julie and Dennis have made Kansas City their home while enjoying time spent with family and friends in Naples, Florida.

Tanya Wilkie

New Hampshire is home to Tanya Wilkie and husband Bob, retired President and CEO of Sugar River Bank in Newport, NH. Tanya, a registered nurse and nurse/educator, has been a community leader for many years. She was President and CEO of Lake Sunapee's Visiting Nurse Association, then transitioned to the Sugar River Valley Regional Technical Center Health Science Technology Program at Newport Middle High School as a nurse/educator, where she implemented student healthcare career programs.

Retiring in 2013, Tanya continues as Trustee Emeritus to New London Hospital and is active in the Lake Sunapee Protective Association, where she is past Board President. She led the capital campaign, "Building Health," successfully raising funds for the Newport Health Center of New London Hospital.

Her sunny disposition and healer's heart were honored as 2017 New London Hospital Grand Marshall of Hospital Days and 2016 Lake Sunapee Chamber of Commerce Community Member of the Year. In 2017, she volunteered as an American Red Cross Disaster Relief RN, covering Hurricane Irma, Florida wildfires, and COVID-19. She and Bob lead active outdoor lives in Sunapee and a turn-of-the-century cottage in Newbury on Lake Sunapee. Their three children and five grandchildren live nearby, each following their parents' example of giving back to their communities and enjoying family time at the lake.

Susan Wright

Susan Wright's contagious enthusiasm for education and people has served her well throughout her own career and as the wife of a college president. Susan worked for Dartmouth College for 31 years in a variety of roles with exposure to both faculty and students, giving her broad institutional reach and enhancing the lives of many. Her husband, Jim Wright, the 16th President of Dartmouth, is an esteemed history professor and academic administrator who spent his entire 40-year professional career there.

After giving up her position in the dean of students' office when Jim was named President in 1998, Susan was asked to direct the Montgomery Fellows Program for distinguished visitors, a job she cherished that complemented her role as President's spouse. Jim and Susan retired in 2009. He has continued academic pursuits as a professor emeritus and book author, while Susan continues to positively impact their community as a docent at the Dartmouth Museum of Art. She also sits on the board of Colby-Sawyer College in New London.

Susan holds an undergraduate degree in History from Vassar College and a master's degree in Education from Stanford University, yet above all, she values her status as grandmother most.

Beth Zollar

Beth Zollar is a multi-faceted businesswoman with decades of extensive industry-sector and functional experience. She is a high-energy, creative, accountable leader with a proven track record in retail consumer and luxury goods, management and technology consulting, and most recently economic /community development and urban planning. Currently, she is a master's candidate at USC Sol Price School of Public Policy, with focus on urban planning and policy. Her newly launched equity-driven urban strategy consultancy focuses on economic development, stakeholder engagement, public/private partnerships, and urban planning.

As an executive in Fortune 500s, Beth has comprehensive depth in sales, marketing, branding, strategic planning, and executive management. Her positions in a technology startup provided a broad base of consulting experience from clients in healthcare, retail, finance, and technology. As an entrepreneur, with successful regional lifestyle stores, she gained valuable experience in business creation and hands-on operation.

Her twenty years as an innovative community leader focusing on women's and children's issues solidified her advocacy for equity-driven solutions for the most vulnerable community members. Her non-profit board experiences built a knowledge base for creating strategic public/private partnerships and extensive fund development plans. Her recent work in affordable housing and homelessness catalyzed her focus on innovative economic and community-based solutions.

Bill Zollars, Beth's spouse, is the former chairman, president, and chief executive officer of YRC Worldwide (now known as YRC Freight) and currently serves as the lead independent director of Cerner.

CHAPTER TWO

What We Found

Six themes emerged from the interviews with our study group, collected and organized, so that you may experience their transitions while perhaps giving voice to a few of your inner thoughts and expectations as you contemplate a retirement transition with your spouse/partner.

1. Prepare for a range of emotions
2. Retain your identity
3. Communicate authentically
4. Rekindle your relationship and attend to your health
5. Prioritize family and friends
6. Enjoy the new season

1. PREPARE FOR A RANGE
OF EMOTIONS

2. RETAIN YOUR
IDENTITY

3. COMMUNICATE
AUTHENTICALLY

1. PREPARE FOR A RANGE OF EMOTIONS

How is your spouse handling the transition? "At this point very well. It only took about 20 years."

The study group experienced a range of emotions when they learned their spouse/partner was retiring. The circumstances of the retirement and the executive's reaction were important factors in the specific—and at times, conflicting—emotions felt, and included an initial resistance to the change. The participants reported feeling unease, especially about how retirement would affect the lives they had built for themselves.

Letting Go

Citing their partner's mindset and emotional state as a leading factor, the spouse/partners interviewed expressed feeling uneasiness and anticipation as part of discussions on downsizing and simplifying, continued work, and redefining roles and expectations. Participants shared the emotions they both experienced when adjusting to the fact of and the actual retirement.

What I found was that he was uncertain, and that made me feel like I was a little bit out to sea. It's like "well, dude, you're supposed to be guiding us here." So, it was a little bit uncomfortable for a while. Like, where are we going with all of this? So, there was six months to a year of uncertainty and unease. Now it seems to be settling down. Sort of the magical place where all the pieces are kind of gently falling from the sky.

I had the tougher time. You think he would have had the harder time, but he had people asking him to do things.

I had a health issue. I was diagnosed with cancer and he took a leave of absence and decided to retire after that. I think also he was ready to retire. I think the health issue was challenging. Not that he wasn't used to big jobs, but the timing of the health issue coincided with his

4. REKINDLE YOUR RELATIONSHIP
AND ATTEND TO YOUR HEALTH

5. PRIORITIZE FAMILY
AND FRIENDS

6. ENJOY THE
NEW SEASON

retirement. He didn't know what it was, but he was ready to move onto something else.

I was happy to see him let go of the stress of the job; the long hours, the travel, being expected to show up and entertain customers.

It's shifting, everything is shifting, life is shifting, everything. Recognize it's not just you and your retirement, it's both of you.

Shortly after he retired, we ran into a work colleague of his. He asked my husband rather wistfully: do you miss feeling important? The question surprised him, but if he was to be honest, the answer was yes! He was used to being ON all the time and it was hard to turn down the volume.

I believe he was not ready for full retirement. I could not see him being happy not having work, because work for him included deep friendships. He'd been in the industry since he was 22 years old. He was not going to be one that would have been able to cut it off and say I'm done.

I think most executives are used to being busy and it was impossible for my spouse to just stop.

He wanted to move on. He didn't know how well his health would hold out and he wanted to have some healthy retirement years. The work just didn't light him up anymore. It was too stressful to think about getting up at 4 in the morning and traveling across the country and getting the same work done he used to get done.

I was excited for him to explore other things. I'd say we disagreed a little bit on how that would shake out. It was pretty quiet; a few people knew that he was willing to look at other things. I felt like there would be many more opportunities to evaluate.

In terms of my involvement, this was her retirement and her timing, and I was fine with whatever she elected to do.

....

Could we have made the transition to retirement less painful? At first, it was excruciating for him. His career was his life. He cut the tail off the puppy with a cleaver, but within six months he wasn't even thinking about his job anymore. In remembering this period, I think he handled it well. He had tried to retire for several years, but the company resisted. In order to retire fully vested, the separation from the company had to be amicable. A lot of emotional preparation happened in those years of waiting for the company to allow his retirement.

....

Tying Up Loose Ends

Participants reported a need for closure as their executive turned from their career responsibilities to possibilities going forward. Leaving the job well—finishing in a way that honored both the executive and company was reported to be important in the adjustment to this first next season.

....

Because his entire department was outsourced, he was still spending a good bit of time getting his employees where they needed to be. I think he measured some of his transition success on how many people he was able to help find a place.

....

One of his challenges when he was working is that he had so many other interests and was often very frustrated that he couldn't get to them. So, I had no concerns when he retired that he'd be sitting around wondering what to do with himself. That was a problem that we did not have, so that's good. He has a wine collection, he is a photographer, he reads prolifically, he works out and is involved with some community work. He is just interested in all kinds of things. Being bored or restless was not going to be a problem.

....

4. REKINDLE YOUR RELATIONSHIP
AND ATTEND TO YOUR HEALTH

5. PRIORITIZE FAMILY
AND FRIENDS

6. ENJOY THE
NEW SEASON

At the beginning of his retirement, he was busy networking and doing some consulting on his own. He reached out to some friends who retired. He was always looking ahead, getting involved.

Headhunters were calling and he was calling headhunters.

Downsizing

Our study group cited impending retirement as a time to consider decluttering and selling the family home as a means of simplifying life and preparing for the next season.

One of the things I'm dealing with now is the downsizing of our home. That is part of moving into the next phase. Getting rid of all the stuff you acquired. That's taken up a lot of my time, going through and that's kind of painful. I was thinking, "why did we get so much stuff?" To me it's so unimportant.

Downsize, really downsize. What I've found talking to other people: your kids don't want any of this stuff. They have lives of their own and they can't deal with your stuff. We had so much stuff our kids were panicking, and they said to their dad, look, we don't know how we can do this. It was very complicated, so we started 3 years ago and we're still at it. That's my biggest thing; really start preparing yourself 10 years earlier and go through your stuff with somebody that you trust and know. Find out what you can do with what you've got. My husband is mostly doing it himself.

Luckily, we were mid-move and I think that helped because we were so busy, we'd bought a newly constructed home, so we had to make many choices and then furnish it. That kept us quite busy; it was more than just unpacking boxes.

The Letdown

Our study group reported feeling a letdown in two ways: a release from a fast-paced, conscribed cadence of life and the emotional repercussions of expectations both fulfilled and surprising.

You have to expect a letdown. It is exhilarating to be in this position. It's great to be out of this position. It was the first time in I don't know how many years that suddenly, your time is not scripted. The events don't define your time. You don't have to go here, here, here, like everything is scheduled, suddenly you're not scheduled; that is really liberating. But, it's also not as exciting.

What was hard for me: the kids went off to college and then my husband retired. I felt I had no alone time. I had looked forward to that time. I was a little bit resentful.

Having him home held me to the house. I was used to leaving and running errands and doing my own thing in my own time. It felt like I had someone at home just waiting for me to get home.

I saw a husband who was afraid. It's one thing to talk the talk but another thing to pull the plug. I needed to be patient and we talked about retirement A LOT. It was the focal point in our conversations within our marriage for quite a number of years.

It was great to have no more phone calls in the middle of the night and phone calls on vacation. I was happy to have him join me for family functions and other responsibilities.

He left behind unfinished business which was hard on him.

It is the single most profound shift at so many levels that they need to not underestimate it. It's more than just saying goodbye to a career, it is an internal shift of getting to know oneself, the executive needs to take full responsibility for getting acquainted with oneself after hiding from

4. REKINDLE YOUR RELATIONSHIP
AND ATTEND TO YOUR HEALTH

5. PRIORITIZE FAMILY
AND FRIENDS

6. ENJOY THE
NEW SEASON

one's inner life. To allow plenty of time for that self to quietly emerge over time. It cannot be done overnight.

At first, he was sleeping in and I resented it, but I knew he was recovering. I didn't want him to feel badly so I wanted to adopt a much more positive attitude—no complaining. He could very easily beat himself up. I was very careful, very sensitive, and tried hard. I tried to process stuff with my friends.

I was very concerned that the end of his career would mean a significant curtailment of my activities. In the beginning, I was correct. His desire to serve on a mission was not on any to-do list I had. At some point I realized I was on board that train whether I liked it or not, and as it turned out, serving was a tremendous experience. Fortunately, the seeds of the not-for-profit project he founded were germinated during that mission.

I'm just not as involved in his career now. There are not as many demands on me. Even though he is busy with his three different boards, there's not such a demand for me. I go to the Christmas dinners or when they have a spouse trip or something like that. Or I'll go out for dinner, I'm there when I'm needed, but I'm not needed as much.

There's always more to do if he wants to. I feel like there's a level of deflation from their perspective too because I think they think the phone is going to be ringing off the hook. While he did have some nice opportunities, I don't think it's ever as much as you think it's going to be. You know, we're all expendable, and I think people have the idea that they're not.

After he transitioned, my role was sometimes just to let him talk about what he wanted to do in the future and what he thought we should try and do; how much he wanted to work. There were times he would act like he missed going into work every day, but then that subsided quickly. I think he really enjoyed the time.

It was difficult because he had all these plans and I still had the things I wanted to do.

The Pause

Participants shared that they felt pressure from family, friends, and colleagues for their retiring executive to formulate and share a definitive plan for retirement—to know quickly what was next for them. The study group felt conflicted by this pressure, although they, themselves, felt uneasy in the flux of not knowing. At the same time, some acknowledged the need for their executives to slow down, attend to health, and not rush into the next "thing."

At MyNextSeason, we call this the Pause, a time of discernment and exploration. A pause can be as long as needed to recover from the rigors of a high-powered career and attend to family and other priorities.

Make sure you take the first two years slowly. Anything you can do to slow life down is helpful. Spend time considering options, because any decisions that you do make will work only for the short term.

He started his own business, and I felt like he approached it in a way that was very corporate, which is good. At the same time, he may not have given himself the kind of rest and permission to rest that he could have from a health perspective.

Having him have that time and space to himself after he retired, and I kept working, let him really figure out what he wanted to do, what he enjoyed, what worked best for him. I think that's a key ingredient. If the spouse is trying to figure things out, its good not to be around to always be the one making social plans and working things out. There's somewhat of an expectation that the planning is just going to continue. With downtime during the week, he figured out what he wanted to do, what he enjoyed, what worked best for him. Once he did that, I retired!

4. REKINDLE YOUR RELATIONSHIP
AND ATTEND TO YOUR HEALTH

5. PRIORITIZE FAMILY
AND FRIENDS

6. ENJOY THE
NEW SEASON

*I apparently began making suggestions about types of things he could
do, places he could go or individuals he could network with. I think he
read that as he wasn't moving fast enough along this transition curve,
and he got a little bit snitty. He's a great communicator, so he said, "you
know, I need to do this in my time and when you start talking about
me interviewing here and me doing this and me doing that, it makes
me feel like you're rushing me and we've got a year, so I just need you to
allow me to go through this process."*

I think he really enjoyed this time.

*There's that immediate "what am I going to do with my time?" Pretty
quickly he said, "here's a chance to reset." Luckily, we were financially
able to make that choice. Not everyone will have that freedom. That is
a big blessing.*

*Anytime you give yourself the opportunity to explore what gives you life
and what gives you energy and then you go do it, the soul-searching
time is never wasted.*

*I think it takes a while to come off that high of a constant need to
respond to somebody and a constant demand of your time. I think it
takes 3–6 months to get off that roller coaster completely.*

*With just having a few weeks between the work, I felt like he and
the family would have benefitted from a little more cushion between
picking up something new.*

His retirement has forced me to slow down, too. I've been enjoying that.

*I think we kind of put things on hold, took a breather and a break;
deciding what he wanted to do next, what it would look like. It was
almost like a person taking a sabbatical, kind of catching your breath.
We have to focus.*

WHAT WE FOUND **45**

1. PREPARE FOR A RANGE
OF EMOTIONS

2. RETAIN YOUR
IDENTITY

3. COMMUNICATE
AUTHENTICALLY

2. RETAIN YOUR IDENTITY

"We specialize in different things."

The spouse/partners shared extensively about accommodating the new reality of having their executive home. The need to determine boundaries became clear as each navigated the reality of a calendar with no set meetings and goals. Skills honed to meet the needs of long-held roles were modified to accommodate being physically together in the same space. Expectations were either met or adjusted to support each partner in living as a couple, while redefining and committing to roles. Assumptions were challenged and discoveries made to the betterment of the relationship.

Setting Boundaries

Learning the rhythm of a home with two people present took time, respect, and good senses of humor, according to our study group. Bonuses included the surprise and delight of watching routine chores become the welcome domain of your partner.

You have to start learning boundaries, especially if they're doing something for their work or their career. You have to give them the time and space they need, and I think that was hard for me. I wanted to pop in and talk to him, and I realized I couldn't disturb him anytime I wanted. There are boundaries that I had to learn and respect, especially as he was planning on having a different career post-retirement.

He wanted to get out and see people and talk to people and do things. I did want to do some of that, but I also wanted to spend time on what I was working on. He didn't realize how much time I was spending on these other things.

I got up and went to work. My day was still the same. The only part that seemed different to me was that when I got home, he was usually in the garage when the door went up, not necessarily waiting for me,

4. REKINDLE YOUR RELATIONSHIP
AND ATTEND TO YOUR HEALTH

5. PRIORITIZE FAMILY
AND FRIENDS

6. ENJOY THE
NEW SEASON

but not out of town or busy doing something else. I think that if I were a stay-at-home spouse, it would be totally different, because he would be invading my space. In contrast with what happened, is that when I retire, I'll be invading his space.

My life didn't really change that much. It was probably something he had to figure out, although that last year at the office—he called it his victory lap.

One thing that I think he finds himself a little bit sucked into more than he thought was all the acquaintances and friends that think he has time to help them with architectural projects he did so well in his career. There have been people that asked him to help them, but they don't understand that he has to sketch, to sit down and draw, and think it through. It's not that he doesn't want to do it, but it's taking away from his hobbies. Sometimes people aren't sensitive to that. I think they are almost thinking, "oh, you must need something to do." But that's not really the case with him. He's got plenty of things to do. And I try to intercept some of that. Whenever someone brings it up, I'll make a joke, so they get the message that that's not what he's spending his time doing.

We do some things together, some things separately, and that works for us.

Find something you're interested in. Don't necessarily let him be the one to determine everything that's going on. Keep your identity. Keep yourself involved with things that are important to you, not just both of you.

We had an understanding as to not only what the retiring person is going to do, but what do I want to continue to do.

After he retired, I did not always want to stroke his ego for him.

He has a professional group that meets every week for lunch, and they talk stocks. I've gone to dinner with them and their wives a few times. They are very nice people and I have a nice time at dinner, but I have

1. PREPARE FOR A RANGE
OF EMOTIONS

2. RETAIN YOUR
IDENTITY

3. COMMUNICATE
AUTHENTICALLY

enough friends. Isn't that terrible? This isn't going to be a whole new group of couples that we start doing stuff with. These are his friends, but not people I want to be in my inner circle.

He makes all the arrangements for travel, which is great! We specialize in different things.

When we are home together in our house, he says I closet myself in my office and I do, because I need quiet space around me. He's on the phone all day, making appointments and talking with people. He needs that. If things get too quiet, he'll come into my office to see if we can do something together.

His first year retired was before our teenager could drive, so he started taking him to school. Honestly, that was my job, so I thought "what's going on here?" But I didn't want to not include him, and didn't want him to feel like he wasn't part of the family at all. That was something I had to learn to kind of give up, and learn to compromise on my role as a mom in the house.

I expect him to do more around the house. He makes the bed.

This happened gradually over 2 years, but he does his own laundry now. He just started doing his own. For all those years, I did all our laundry, the kids and his, and then when the kids left, I did his. I don't think he even knew where the hangers were or how to start the washing machine, but he figured it out. He's started loading the dishwasher during the day, so that when I come home from work, I'm not loading his dishes. Because he never did anything like that around the house, which never actually bothered me. He had other things that he did that I didn't do . . .

Before he retired, I went to the grocery store. Now, he likes to go to Costco.

4. REKINDLE YOUR RELATIONSHIP
AND ATTEND TO YOUR HEALTH

5. PRIORITIZE FAMILY
AND FRIENDS

6. ENJOY THE
NEW SEASON

I have commitments independent of him. He comes to the dinners to support me, and we make philanthropic decisions together.

He has a lot of hobbies. He does a lot of volunteer work. It wasn't hard for him to fill the hours. And I kind of kept on doing what I was doing, taking on a few more projects. We seem to meld well. I always believe in separate hobbies. He plays golf and shoots on the weekends: clay birds, trap, and skeet. I play duplicate bridge. I have book club and I like to play tennis.

Creating a Workspace

Participants were unified in reporting the need for separate workspaces. The study group was accustomed to having their own space and routine around the work they do in support of the family unit, including bill-paying, social obligations, and community leadership. For those who undertook projects together, the need for separate offices was just as important as each attended to their respective roles and responsibilities.

He was still consulting for various companies, keeping up-to-speed with everything that was going on at all those companies. So, he kept very busy. Except that he was working from home, so he was in my way!

For the first time in his life, and in his career, he did not have an actual physical location office and all the support that goes with it—and he needed it.

He would just shut the door and that's the best thing to do. I always know if the door is shut, do not go in.

For me it was "Wait a minute! This is my office, so we have to set you up with your own space." So, we right away turned another bedroom into a second office. He's kept a separate office at home ever since, otherwise we would be in each other's hair whenever he was home.

1. PREPARE FOR A RANGE
OF EMOTIONS

2. RETAIN YOUR
IDENTITY

3. COMMUNICATE
AUTHENTICALLY

They need to have a dedicated workspace. I've always said the space issue is important. I think this speaks to relevancy—they need to still feel relevant. Whether it's having an office to do their board stuff or to keep organized or whatever it is. If they don't want to do an off-site office, then definitely have a dedicated space in the house. My spouse has an off-site office.

Administration 101

Another realization was that some executives needed support in learning how to be autonomous and proficient in using technology. The spouse/partners who addressed this issue took measures to teach their loved one basic skills and set clear boundaries.

He had no support staff any longer, and me turning into his secretary just wasn't going to happen! Take orders from him? No way! He had been too busy to learn to type proficiently or use the computer.

Having a younger son, he learned technology quickly. It wasn't that he couldn't do it, he just never had anybody ever show him. He could handle his emails. Now, he does his own PowerPoint presentations. He can book travel and do all that stuff. I never did any of that for him. I wasn't his secretary at home, but I did show him how to do a spreadsheet. He picked it up. It wasn't a big deal.

She didn't have the computer support team for instance, so she would turn to me and say, "my computer isn't working." She wouldn't know what to do. Or she would say, "can you fax me this or fax that, and I didn't know how to use the fax machine." Anticipating the kinds of things your spouse might be used to getting that they would not be getting when they retire might help.

The combination of not having administrative support and not having technology training early in his career, or for that matter anytime in his career, meant he didn't have the skills he needed when he retired.

4. REKINDLE YOUR RELATIONSHIP
AND ATTEND TO YOUR HEALTH

5. PRIORITIZE FAMILY
AND FRIENDS

6. ENJOY THE
NEW SEASON

Establishing a Routine

Some found it difficult for their retiring partner to let go of years-in-the-making routines. Planning activities in advance helped.

In terms of expectations, I think by personality, he is very focused on what he's doing or what he needs to be doing. By getting up and going to the office for 39 years and doing what he had to do, I think that's just the pattern of life he got into. I wished and maybe hoped that he would shift gears a little bit and be more interested in doing things together; he still really follows his prior pattern; he gets up, after breakfast he goes into his den, gets on the computer or takes care of things he's interested in or sets up appointments or whatever. It's almost like he's just got his office at home now.

My spouse needs a routine. I initiate activities, plan them in advance and communicate the plans. We don't do spontaneity.

Have a plan for what you want to do next. And your plan could even be for just the next year, such as: I'm going to play golf or play with grandkids or reconnect with old buddies. I am going to do those things I haven't been able to do.

It was kind of a jolt to me to have my husband, be at home all the time. I was used to my world of volunteering and doing things at school and being with my girlfriends for lunch. All of sudden I had him in the house and I thought maybe I needed to be around more to see if he wanted to have lunch; to see if he wanted to do something with me. It changed my life very dramatically in that regard. I was used to him leaving and coming home at 7. Now I had somebody in the house with me.

Calendaring

It took time to get the hang of maintaining calendars—two individual calendars and one combined. Without administrative support, the retiring executive was reactivating a skill; remembering to coordinate with one another took time and some scheduling mistakes.

It's much easier to plan calendars—we talk about our plans and commitments; what we do separately and what we do together, and what we do to support each other.

We work at coordinating our calendars, but we don't have a lot of experience. Now, suddenly, our calendars aren't driven by the have-to-do's. It's full of freedom and we have never created our own calendar. We try to plan well. We have sit-downs so we can cover like, "oh, you're going out of town or I'm doing this?!" We stay in touch with what's going on and planning our fun because, next thing you know, I've made my commitments and he's made his, and sometimes they can be quite different. So, we have learned to say like, "let's plan this"—like we're doing a bike trip in June over in Tuscany, but it doesn't happen without sitting down and planning.

He was used to an administrative assistant who set his schedule. He was used to having everything laid out in front of him, appointments, this and that and the other. He looked at my calendar one day and he said, "I think you could be a little more organized with this." I remember turning and looking at him sideways, saying, "I've done pretty well all this time without you here telling me that my calendar could be a little more organized, or how my day could flow a little more easily."

I suggest we go to the museum today or see that show tomorrow night or whatever. He does not make any plans for us; he hasn't gotten that, after nine years, we could be doing more together. Maybe now he can make time to focus on the other things we could do.

Sharing Space

Having someone else around more than ever before created challenges for our study group. Some participants hoped for household duties

4. REKINDLE YOUR RELATIONSHIP
AND ATTEND TO YOUR HEALTH

5. PRIORITIZE FAMILY
AND FRIENDS

6. ENJOY THE
NEW SEASON

and chores to be shared, and all had adjustment when that did—or did not—happen. Having another person home, with the attendant comings and goings, was a dynamic that took some getting used to.

Having him home created a different dynamic between the two of us, just because he was there all the time. It wasn't necessarily negative; it was just different.

There were some days where it was like, "you need to go get a job." If I happened to be home, I thought, "you need to leave." I was not used to having my spouse at home when I was home. Not that I was always home, which was great, because I had my own business, but on the days that I would be home, or the days I would come home early, there was definitely more focus from his perspective on what was going on in the house, what was going on in our teenager's life. And those became annoyances. I thought to myself, "this is my realm." Even though I have my own life and my own business, the house was never equally shared. It was always under my domain. So, whatever happened with the house, with the kids or the pets—that was my charge. When he started encroaching on that, it became annoying. There were times, well, we had to work that out and figure it out. I didn't want to not include him, but it was more of retraining on my part; I had to learn to include him.

Having somebody you're bumping into at the fridge in the morning and you're not used to having them there—that was a big adjustment. I was used to having my house to myself during the day, and all of a sudden, I've got somebody else at the kitchen sink washing blueberries? I was going to wash those blueberries! We just have learned how to navigate the day.

There are adjustments that you figure out, especially having a person at home who might be working out of a home office all day. The house was my zone.

WHAT WE FOUND **53**

1. PREPARE FOR A RANGE
OF EMOTIONS

2. RETAIN YOUR
IDENTITY

3. COMMUNICATE
AUTHENTICALLY

At home I thought he might start taking care of the pool or some of the things around the house that I always hired out. I have kidded him that I thought he'd become the pool boy, but he has not become the pool boy yet!

Let's Do Lunch—or Not

Interestingly, dormant culinary aspirations surprised many spouse/partners when their newly retired executive started whipping up meals and reorganizing the kitchen. This was one area where it took some time to get comfortable and let go.

I joke about this, but it was very real. One of the bigger challenges that we worked out very quickly was the kitchen. The kitchen had been my domain and I had no problem with that. My spouse functions in a kitchen totally differently than how I do. Initially, he thought it was helpful to me to fix his own lunch. It became apparent very quickly that it was more work for me to clean up after him and put the kitchen back in the way I like it to be. It was easier to just fix his lunch myself assuming the that I was home too.

My role as a spouse has changed. I wanted to be a homemaker when I was raising children. Now he is fully capable of making his own sandwich. I do cook, but I don't consider it to be my role. However, if I didn't go to the grocery store, he would starve to death.

A friend of mine said, "don't ever offer to make lunch, because you'll be stuck with that job every day." And I thought, "well that's kind of rude if I'm making lunch for myself, certainly I can make lunch for him." But then I learned what she meant.

That was one specific thing we had to adjust to fairly quickly. He would sprawl all over the kitchen with stuff and not pick up and put away as

4. REKINDLE YOUR RELATIONSHIP
AND ATTEND TO YOUR HEALTH

5. PRIORITIZE FAMILY
AND FRIENDS

6. ENJOY THE
NEW SEASON

he went along. He'd eat his meal and then put things away. That didn't work for me.

One of my husband's great loves in life is eating well, and so he wants us to have three sit-down meals a day. It's a struggle for me, because I'm used to eating on the run most of the time."

Perhaps you should be gathering data from him. A recent low point was when I left for the grocery store and asked what he wanted. In reply, he named his favorite frozen meals.

Since I was very reluctant to cook three meals a day, and he's a much better cook than I am, he now cooks most of the time, which is nice. That part works out well.

He took over the cooking. Now that was kind of a shock.

Being True to Yourself . . .

Our study participants had successfully built satisfying and separate lives from their hard-charging counterparts. Some worked fulltime and all carried primary responsibility for running the home and caring for family and friends. Some chose to continue working fulltime so their executive would have the time and space to figure out what was next for them. While adjustments were made, there was recognition and support for sharing the care of the home and family.

As each new opportunity rolls around, you have to evaluate: is that part of my plan, do I want to do that? As each year rolls around, what are the things I want to accomplish this year? I think those are the things that are most helpful for me. If there were important friendships involved in that, finding ways to maintain them.

It's been six years, and only now am I beginning to get back a sense of who I am and what I want to do with my time.

1. PREPARE FOR A RANGE
OF EMOTIONS

2. RETAIN YOUR
IDENTITY

3. COMMUNICATE
AUTHENTICALLY

I am able to show up for things in person, able to pursue that a little more, and able to think of my transition from being the primary caregiver of the children at home to my children being more independent. Plus, with my husband around, I can think of the things that I want to pursue now locally and internationally.

We are in a season of him being more engaged in day-to-day family in a way he hadn't been able to. Now he is able to support me and the family by having more flexible time when I want to do other things. I think certainly there will be another season when we both have other things we want to pursue, but we haven't quite gotten to that phase yet.

You just have to have some passion.

Stay upbeat, and if you had something that you were interested in doing before that you never had time, just try it.

Now I've got the freedom to both fail and succeed on a more significant scale.

I don't dream. I do. I make to-do lists. I love mornings. The only thing I enjoy is watching the sun rise, otherwise I need to be doing.

When your spouse retires, and you have supported your partner's career, you might suffer a void in your life, an amount of time that can become a gap, that you spent living out the role of supporting spouse. Find your interests, pursue new ideas now, because without all the entertaining and travel, you are going to have some time on your hands with which to do something interesting. Consider that amount of time you spent in that support role and how you want to fill that up and be prepared for it. It's almost like a kid leaving for college, I guess. You have to figure out how you're going to fill up that time.

4. REKINDLE YOUR RELATIONSHIP
AND ATTEND TO YOUR HEALTH

5. PRIORITIZE FAMILY
AND FRIENDS

6. ENJOY THE
NEW SEASON

From my perspective, in a way, I was glad he had plenty to keep him busy. I was already doing things that I had been busy with—with the kids, school, and volunteer commitments. I wasn't expected to drop everything now that he was dropping his career and retiring.

Reach out to organizations that already exist and really need you. I think people need to feel and know that they have something to give.

Think about little things you want to do that have either made you happy in the past or you've never tried and think you want to.

Hopefully you know what your passion is before your spouse retires—and hopefully your spouse has a passion, too. It's probably too late if you don't know what you want, if you lack passion, if you don't have any plans.

Have your own agenda—make it your own. Your spouse has successfully done that with their career, now it's the trailing spouse's time to do what they want to do, and your spouse can be the supportive spouse.

One of the real positives is that he has never minded my doing the things that I do. He is very open to my schedule; I keep him informed: you know tomorrow I have a meeting, I'll be back at such-and-such.

I've learned through all this, don't place the blame for anything that I am not already wanting to do with my own life. It's so easy and selfish to look at each other and blame one another and say the retirement should go faster or better. What I've learned is, every day I wake up and think it's my life, it's my script, what do I want to do with it? Ultimately, it's my job to take care of my own life. My hope is that my partner would really be able to channel whatever he gained from his career of more than three decades as he finds his new life. And only he can do that. I can't do that for him.

My personal belief is that I need to look for ways I can continue to grow and learn.

1. PREPARE FOR A RANGE
OF EMOTIONS

2. RETAIN YOUR
IDENTITY

3. COMMUNICATE
AUTHENTICALLY

I just made the decision I need to move on with my life. It was a very private decision I made. I let him know that I figured out my path, even though I didn't know what he was going to do.

I stumbled onto a unique four-year project that challenged me immensely and became quite popular, even around the world. I had no idea I would become something of a minor celebrity. He was supportive throughout and answered uncountable technical questions. He even encouraged me to submit to interviews when I wanted to remain anonymous.

. . . While Pursuing Life Together

Purpose drove the choices our study group made with their significant others. The participants reported looking forward to pursuing activities, classes, and outings together as a couple now that there was time to enjoy it. Some undertook philanthropic projects together, and others participated in the activities of the other, such as golf or volunteering. The study group felt that investing in your own interests and activities as well as coming together for shared activities was a powerful combination that fueled both themselves and the relationship.

We talked and we had no desire to sit around. We wanted to have purpose in life. I think purpose is the big deal. Find a purpose if you don't have one. You've got to have something to get up for.

We're working together on this philanthropic project, so that's been a real learning, actually kind of a rocky road. How he works and how I work on projects are two different things. That's been interesting.

Both people need to have separate interests, and interests or projects together. So, you need to be both independent and yet share a life together. I think it's really important that you want to come together and talk and share ideas. You have to do things independently, so you

4. REKINDLE YOUR RELATIONSHIP
AND ATTEND TO YOUR HEALTH

5. PRIORITIZE FAMILY
AND FRIENDS

6. ENJOY THE
NEW SEASON

have something to talk about together. You have to have some common interests.

. . . .

We never said, "oh yes, when we retire, we're definitely doing X." We're living each day to achieve the things we want to achieve and hopefully help some other people along the way.

. . . .

It is important that that my spouse feels that he has a purpose and like he is contributing and achieving the things he wants in his life.

. . . .

He had all kinds of plans upon retirement that involved me, and I still felt like I had a full list of responsibilities.

. . . .

I think it's a nice time to be able to explore couple-like things you could do together; something you've always been putting off, or go to cooking school together, or learn to play golf together, or do something together because you probably didn't have that time before.

. . . .

We are both on the Friends of the Library board in our small community.

. . . .

Maybe it's time for me to go back to work, and for my spouse, who is retiring, to take a bigger role at home, whether it be paid or unpaid.

. . . .

Life goes on. He had golf. I decided I was going to get into golf, and I had two dogs that I loved walking. I don't know if you have to have big lofty goals.

. . . .

For me, when my spouse retired, I continued to work fulltime for another year. That year gave him the time to reinvent himself. And he truly did do that.

. . . .

I am supported in my own separate activities, as well as activities we do together.

. . . .

1. PREPARE FOR A RANGE
OF EMOTIONS

2. RETAIN YOUR
IDENTITY

3. COMMUNICATE
AUTHENTICALLY

We may have had a few rougher spots early on, but it's smooth now. In part, I think we both lived independent lives, but we always come together every evening. We have our own interests and activities and sometimes they coincide, you know if we're going to play golf together or just with a group or each other.

We're working on a project together, but we still have separate roles. We keep a division of labor—I think that is important.

I think being willing to voice your own dreams and own concerns— in a way, this might be the first time that your spouse has really had the opportunity to support those along the way. Certainly, he had always been supportive of me, but because of our roles, his schedule, and corporate relocations, there wasn't much opportunity for me to be supported by him. Looking into a transition, certainly there's more time where it can be a collaborative effort, or him helping me think through some of my transition opportunities.

3. COMMUNICATE AUTHENTICALLY

"You've got to be honest with each other and know it's not all about you."

The spouse/partners reported that good conversations and planning laid the foundation for calibrating expectations for the first season after retirement. By having important discussions about needs, expectations, and dreams, they felt they were investing in a partnership that allowed for individual and shared interests with the capacity to take care of family as needed.

Sharing Well

The spouse/partners shared that different emotions elicited during this transition affected both parties in different ways and needed to be

4. REKINDLE YOUR RELATIONSHIP
AND ATTEND TO YOUR HEALTH

5. PRIORITIZE FAMILY
AND FRIENDS

6. ENJOY THE
NEW SEASON

discussed. Sharing thoughts, ideas, and feelings in a caring and honest manner created an environment of trust and collaboration that led to a strengthening of the partnership. Giving feedback helped both spouse/partner and executive let go and stay forward-focused.

Coming together and getting on the same page together is healthy for the relationship. I think using that time of stress to kind of turn to each other, as opposed to looking for something outside the marriage, is probably a very healthy thing for your marriage for the future.

Recently I've started to say to him, "Hey, you're retired, you're not responsible anymore, we've given enough years to that company, so that's it, no more conversation today." I'm kind of feeling like it's time to hang that one up a bit. You know, we do talk about other things of course, and I make a point to make sure we're talking about other things.

We talk things out in a partnership. You support when you can support and need to support.

You've got to be honest with each other and know it's not all about you. I think that probably happens a lot of times with the spouse. They're indignant or they feel a certain way because this has happened to them, but they've got to realize they are a pebble in a lake, it affects everyone, all the way to the children and the extended family.

Think hard about what you want and then share that with your spouse. Let your spouse do the same. Share those things honestly and listen with all your heart. If you are not on the same page at all, consider where you could compromise. Be open to the idea of getting counseling for help. And don't lose your sense of humor! You will need it!

We thought it made sense to talk about what day-to-day life will look like. And then we let things evolve.

1. PREPARE FOR A RANGE
OF EMOTIONS

2. RETAIN YOUR
IDENTITY

3. COMMUNICATE
AUTHENTICALLY

You pray, you try to do your best, you consider each other's feelings, and you listen to each other. Many times people just don't listen. We sit down and we talk about it.

I feel like my perspective right now is committed to creating an environment of sharing. It is important with kids at home to consider how parenting decisions are made. Before he retired, I made all those decisions and that was what it was. To have to consult somebody about what they felt or maybe we had a difference of opinion; that was new territory for me.

Listening Well

Many spouse/partners listened to their retiring executives' thoughts—the anxiety and reactions, ideas, and dreams—as their executive transitioned. They found their executives had a hard time letting go and choosing what might be next. Some found it a good time to share as well—others found support elsewhere for their angst until their partner had settled in a bit.

They're already feeling a level of anxiety sitting where they are, even though they try to look like they're not. When a well-meaning spouse starts jumping in with all those things, they think are helpful, they may misinterpret that as just not quite as beneficial as it was intended. So, let them be the initiator of whatever it is that they ask.

I think you should let your spouse talk as much as they want. For a while you have to expect that your spouse cannot support your feelings; you have to support them and theirs. Get your support elsewhere at first.

It's not that as individuals we must be able to talk about interesting things, but we certainly need to know how to listen and how to positively contribute to a conversation so that all are engaged and involved.

4. REKINDLE YOUR RELATIONSHIP
AND ATTEND TO YOUR HEALTH

5. PRIORITIZE FAMILY
AND FRIENDS

6. ENJOY THE
NEW SEASON

I wish for him to have learned a few better listening skills. To sit down and say, "Hey, how is this impacting you?"

After he transitioned, my role was sometimes just to let him talk about what he wanted to do in the future and what he thought we should try and do; how much he wanted to work. There were times he would act like he missed going into work, but then that subsided pretty quickly.

Dreaming Together

Travel, mission trips, joining each other in what once were solo activities, were topics of discussion—dreams shared as discussions took place before, during, and after retirement. Some couples had a bucket list and others had a list of practical chores and activities to accomplish. The study group called out dreaming together as a unique part of sharing and listening. It involved future planning, tied to common interests and hopes for what could be, formed early in the relationships.

We had the conversation about what we want to do now with our lives.

Certain travel, certain trips have been planned; talked about that a lot. It would have been good to talk about doing simple things like, "let's drive up into the country today or go to the museum this afternoon," and kind of put that out there as a wish list of expectations. There must have been some of that, but I don't remember how much we actively talked about that.

I just thought the best thing for me is to follow my heart and create what I want to create. So, by the time he retired, that dream was already moving. Now there are other dreams I still have. I still have room to dream. But the thing that surprised me, is I want to make sure my dreams are in sync with his so that we're not dreaming in different directions.

1. PREPARE FOR A RANGE
OF EMOTIONS

2. RETAIN YOUR
IDENTITY

3. COMMUNICATE
AUTHENTICALLY

It is hard for him to focus more on the things we could be doing together.

When he was ready to start dreaming, he didn't dream by himself. We talked about where we'd like to go and how long we'd like to stay in this house and what's the next place and is there a next place; you know, those kinds of things. We love to travel; where's our next trip? We love to do mission work. That for us did not happen until later that first year.

Our dreams we have dreamt all along. We've had all sorts of conversations and continue to talk about me joining him in his thing when I retire.

4. REKINDLE YOUR RELATIONSHIP AND ATTEND TO YOUR HEALTH

"We have this whole wonderful opportunity to explore new things together."

Without exception, our study group spoke of the importance of enjoying their executive and anticipated spending time together. Some spoke of getting to know one another and rediscovering the attributes of their retiring executive that drew them together initially. For many, assessing their health status and committing to getting healthier was an important part of this next phase of life.

Redefining the Partnership

One spouse/partner communicated how it is important to continue to like one another throughout the marriage and into retirement, which reflected the feelings of many of the spouse/partners. Almost all shared the view that retirement presents a wonderful opportunity to explore new things together. We heard frequently that the marriage would be redefined in this new season.

4. REKINDLE YOUR RELATIONSHIP
AND ATTEND TO YOUR HEALTH

5. PRIORITIZE FAMILY
AND FRIENDS

6. ENJOY THE
NEW SEASON

He relaxed more. I had time to really talk to him and see the person that I married. I got to reacquaint with that person and find out that we still loved each other.

The nice thing is we always had a very trusting relationship and always relied on each other's judgment.

I don't feel like it's all dumped on me to be responsible for everything. I think it tends to be more of a partnership when you're both home some.

You have to kind of prepare and try to maintain a certain respect and support and love that will carry over to each season as you go on. I'm very fortunate, we have a good marriage, but we've certainly been through ups and downs like everybody else and you know it's not easy.

My husband is high-energy. It's kind of hard to keep up with.

The marriage is probably going to have to be redefined. People need room to get to know one another in a new way. If they think it's just about a career shift, it is so much more than that. Expect unexpected emotions to arise such as depression and edginess. These are welcome "friends" that are telling us something about ourselves, and it can be worked through so that something new can emerge eventually.

I just feel like it's nice to have a friend always by your side if you want to do something with them. He's not always available, but we work it out. And I love it that I get chauffeured everywhere. Where I get my hair colored, he gets his haircut! So, this can really serve as a life lesson. I mean, we still have our moments, I don't want it to sound all rosy, rosy. On the whole, I think it's worked better than I ever would have expected.

We still enjoy the physical part of the marriage, which I think is very important.

1. PREPARE FOR A RANGE
OF EMOTIONS

2. RETAIN YOUR
IDENTITY

3. COMMUNICATE
AUTHENTICALLY

He does more to really help me than he ever did when we were both working. And then I think you have less stress and rigmarole. I think the two of you just figure it out a little more. I don't feel like it's all dumped on me to be responsible for everything. I think it tends to be more of a partnership when you're both home some.

He is my hero and he is there for me and I am there for him, no matter what.

Renewing the Relationship

Many spouse/partners cited a strong connection and feeling supported as keys to renewing the partnership. Communicating, prioritizing each other, and being flexible and understanding eased the transition and set realistic expectations as the couples settled into a new chapter in their partnership.

I think everything we've done together has been mutually beneficial. I think it continues that way in retirement. Do I feel supported? I certainly feel supported. She has picked up a lot of the tasks I did when she was working. In some ways I'm doing less than I was before, because she's been home and doing a lot of it herself.

He said, "I'm tired of being in the lead, I'm happy to support you." And that's what he's done.

I still feel that he has a strong executive voice when I challenge him on certain things, such as when he tries to make a decision alone that affects us both. It's difficult because he's so used to making the decisions and moving forward. There are times when I challenge him, and I think "wow! I am talking to this executive right now and I am challenging him, and I can feel the fumes coming out of his nose." We're working through this as a married couple.

4. REKINDLE YOUR RELATIONSHIP
AND ATTEND TO YOUR HEALTH

5. PRIORITIZE FAMILY
AND FRIENDS

6. ENJOY THE
NEW SEASON

He was very respectful of my time and life that I had before retirement.

Be willing to work together on things that are hard and view this work as a positive rather than something that can be draining or not comfortable at the time. In the end, it has many dividends to pay forward for what this new life is going to be like long-term. Whether they go back to work in a new way or if they choose a traditional retirement, that stronger relationship that you build is beneficial.

When we were working, we checked email, we always checked our phones. Now we don't, we just don't. We do it once a day. It's really kind of nice to have this newfound freedom that you don't need to be plugged in and checking your messages, just enjoy being outside.

Practicing Patience

Patience was a key element in adapting to the changing dynamics of the partnership.

Even though our retirement has gone well, it does take a certain amount of patience, and that is just something you practice daily.

For me, for the stage of life we're in; he's at the end of a successful career; I trust in the success that he had. He is not going to all of a sudden fall flat on his face, because that's not who he is, that wouldn't have gotten him where the was in the company. Trust and patience would be the two top things that helped me.

Investing in Your Health

A number of participants had survived health scares, and in some instances, that determined the timing of their spouse/partner's retirement. Many feared for their retiring executive, remembering health issues and shortened retirements of friends and relatives,

1. PREPARE FOR A RANGE
OF EMOTIONS

2. RETAIN YOUR
IDENTITY

3. COMMUNICATE
AUTHENTICALLY

especially their fathers. Virtually all prioritized exercise to maintain health, relieve stress, and look good.

My only fear, which is really silly, is health. You know, we are both really healthy now, but I remember that when his dad retired, he died 2 years later.

Our focus was my health for a year. It's like we had a project. We retired, but here's our new project; it's getting over this cancer. That's what I would compare it to, somebody taking a sabbatical. Maybe that's what people should do when they retire. Look at it before they move onto something, the next thing. Maybe this is my sabbatical to regroup, take a breath and figure out the next step.

Exercising is important. We have a little gym here, and I exercise at the gym for stress relief. That's one of the things we've both done to alleviate stress and deal with it.

There were blessings in the health issues we've had to face. It helped us to slow down and get healthier. It wasn't all bad.

We are lucky we are both active and healthy. Health is a huge part of it. I would say, whatever you can do while you're young to maintain a healthy body and mind, it's worth the investment.

I feel like maybe there's a little bit of an ego there as well. But I think he's happier than ever. I know he's definitely healthier than ever and feels good about where he is. So, that's been a nice opportunity to see him, you know, enjoy life a little bit.

5. PRIORITIZE FAMILY AND FRIENDS

"Life has really changed. I trimmed my social network. We do more things together now."

4. REKINDLE YOUR RELATIONSHIP
AND ATTEND TO YOUR HEALTH

5. PRIORITIZE FAMILY
AND FRIENDS

6. ENJOY THE
NEW SEASON

Excitement was evident among the study group when talking about the opportunity to spend time with family as a couple. Having children in the house and living nearby were cited as factors that helped initially to create structure in the schedule while strengthening family ties in new ways. The majority of the study group cited friendships as important support in this phase of life, and many spoke of how faith and spirituality served as a foundation for their enduring relationship.

Putting Loved Ones First

Our study group enjoyed the newfound spontaneity of gathering with family and friends with their executive. The capacity to be present, together, for children and aging parents in a caretaking role was reported as another benefit. Visiting family drove schedules and facilitated travel plans.

We have our daughter who lives in town, which is wonderful, and we have wonderful friends and new friends who are very dear to us. We are blooming because these people are like the roots of the plant.

You know, when he retired that first year, we still had our youngest in high school. So, we were kind of forced to keep that routine,—you know, you get up, you get your kid off to school. Our daughter was very busy with her activities, and we continued to participate and enjoy her last year of high school. So, that kept him busy the first year.

We make sure we facilitate other family members traveling to visit us, or we go visit them. We want to stay close to our grandchildren. We want to have a good relationship with them, because we feel family is very important.

We just feel really blessed that we have our family close by and we enjoy sharing experiences together. That's truly what we value most at this point in our lives.

When we retired, three out of four of our parents were dying, and it was all very sudden. We became a support team to each other and to each of them. His dad moved in and lived with us. I provided his hospice care as both a registered nurse and daughter-in-law. When my dad became ill and needed our care, we went to Florida. I took care of my dad, and my husband, who has a legal and finance background, took care of all his paperwork. It was overwhelming. It was bad enough to deal with a loved one dying, but suddenly you think of all the stuff you have to take care of before they pass. We came together as a team—a total team. It was truly the best part about my retirement that I retired when I did—we were able to use all of our skills to take care of our loved ones, and we did it together. It was a great experience. Then his mother came to live with us so that we could care for her. We created a team with our children and grandchildren. It's been a four-generation household with loved ones living with us and dying. It was a really good experience for all of us to share.

We are spending time with grandchildren and simplifying.

We have two young adult children. We want them to see what two working parents look like, so it was important that when he was ready, we shared the journey with them. We are very aware that they are watching as they observe how we have handled two careers and now a retirement.

I'd say now, we're much more sharing the load of what goes on in the family as far as both the care and nurturing of our adult children as well as our children at home.

He does more for the kids than he did before, because he has more time and he can do it during the day. Sometimes when our daughter is at work, he'll go over and fix something on her garage or do plumbing in her basement or he'll meet our son for lunch. He's been golfing with the kids on weekends. I do think he's done more with them. It was always family first, but he does more 1:1 things with and for them now.

4. REKINDLE YOUR RELATIONSHIP
AND ATTEND TO YOUR HEALTH

5. PRIORITIZE FAMILY
AND FRIENDS

6. ENJOY THE
NEW SEASON

Reevaluating Friendships

For almost all our study group, personal friendships provided support, companionship, and fun. A number of participants had less time for friendships outside the marriage and family once their executive retired. Other friendships, associated with the job, fell away as there was little-to-no opportunity outside of work to see one another.

When my husband retired, we left a lot of friends behind. I wasn't happy about it. I can't think of anything that I was happy about leaving behind.

The quality of my life certainly didn't change much, but maybe the social interaction on behalf of the company changed. It was more on my own or us as a couple. So, maybe there's some social stigma that goes with that. Your phone doesn't ring as much, that kind of stuff. I think if your ego is tied up in that, then it's going to be a problem.

You will lose acquaintances and friends and maybe even social standing or perceived social standing. You won't be asked to chair as many events, you won't be asked to do this, or to do that, or be on a board. My advice is, don't take it personally. Just realize what it is. It was a role, and that was really all for the company.

Some people may miss the fact that—I don't want to sound funny—but like they were important people. I've heard some people say as soon as they are not an executive anymore, nobody invites them to anything. But that was never really a big part of our lives. We stay involved in what we want to stay involved in, and it hasn't mattered much that he's not a CEO anymore. He doesn't miss the work, and I don't miss the anxiety and burdens that the work caused him.

I am really impressed by so many of the people I have met on boards. I look at these people I serve with and I am so impressed; talk about skills and gifts. I think learning continues to be important, but it probably should be in a new way, in a new setting.

1. PREPARE FOR A RANGE
OF EMOTIONS

2. RETAIN YOUR
IDENTITY

3. COMMUNICATE
AUTHENTICALLY

If you realize some of the people you worked with were only friends because you had to work with them, you can let that go.

We felt it was time to retire. So, we are retired, and we are adjusting. We found that people are very much involved with charity in a hands-on way.

I knew it was time to move on. But what was I going to do? I got an awful lot of opportunities because of who I'm married to. The transition was tough, but I have all kinds of things I am doing now, and I'm very fulfilled.

He has more invitations and friendships with some of his retirement friends and partner friends than he did when he was working. I think he values all his friendships more now that he has time, and makes an effort to participate in things. He doesn't want to miss his lunches with friends on the weekend. One day they flew somewhere for lunch. Before he retired, he would have said, I don't have time to do that.

Life has really changed. I trimmed my social network. I don't do as many things during the day with friends, and I cut down on not-for-profit work. We do more things together now. We travel more.

I tell people his job is to talk on the phone with his friends, to go play with his friends, and to sometimes go to a meeting and do marketing. All of which is pretty darned easy for him, but I think that because it has maintained lots of relationships, it's been a really good thing for him.

A Foundation in Faith

Our study group reported that faith played a role in their relationship, supported them during the turbulence of retirement, and helped their

4. REKINDLE YOUR RELATIONSHIP
AND ATTEND TO YOUR HEALTH

5. PRIORITIZE FAMILY
AND FRIENDS

6. ENJOY THE
NEW SEASON

retiring executive find their way as part of their next season. For some, it became an outlet for service and social interaction.

We have the same faith, and fortunately, we're politically on the same page.

We do not pray together, which I wish that we did, but we don't, but he is a man of prayer. I pray for him daily and I feel like that's still my role. I still do that, but it is different now because we're working on this major community project together. Prayer is part of my role with that.

He had gone from 35 years of having meetings all day and then suddenly, there's nothing on the calendar. Instead, he has his Bible time, and then he would set aside 2–3-hour slots of time in his calendar just like he did when he was at work. This was a part of a plan for him that really helped him focus and soul-search and figure out life.

For me, faith was part of what he needed to figure out what comes next. It was reassuring to see him reading his Bible and daydreaming. You could tell he was thinking and being introspective. For me, it was like "he's got this, he's going to figure this out." It was reassuring.

We really do believe in faith, family, friends, and we have been so blessed to have a wonderful church and a wonderful family. And we have a wonderful group of friends that we've had since we moved here. I think that's important, almost at the core of who you are as a couple.

You just have to build a foundation with God as the center, leaning on him to support you through times of change.

Use what you have, what God's given you for good purpose. But if you don't belong to a church, if you don't have faith, if you're not involved in your community, it is harder.

1. PREPARE FOR A RANGE
OF EMOTIONS

2. RETAIN YOUR
IDENTITY

3. COMMUNICATE
AUTHENTICALLY

6. ENJOY THE NEW SEASON

"This is our season now, but it won't be the last season."

Our twenty-six-member study group was eager to share final thoughts. Rediscovering each other and communicating often and honestly were cited as important for ensuring a strong foundation for the relationship in this season of transition from a hard-driving career into retirement. Consistent feedback included finding support—a friend, a process, a professional—to help ease both partners into a purpose-filled and satisfying first next season.

Hindsight

There is nothing better than the voice of experience, and our participants had much to share. In the end, almost all wished they had planned and prepared for retirement more thoroughly.

Take care of financials. Take care of things maybe 10 years before you retire, and then you don't have it weighing on your head.

Find another purpose in life and be ready to transition to other things that will give you purpose in life.

It's taken a good 2–3 years for him to adjust to retirement. It takes that long, because the changes and adjustments in your life are unbelievable. He's adjusting and I am too. It's very different.

I think in hindsight we should have planned better. We were fortunate, but it was a matter of luck that we came into retirement pretty well set.

I think having a process took fear out of the equation somewhat for me as it gave me assurance; and for him, he knew he needed it to find out where he was headed. So, after having that conversation, it was like, you know, he's got this. I'm going to chill; that is my advice to a spouse whose significant other is going through the process.

4. REKINDLE YOUR RELATIONSHIP
AND ATTEND TO YOUR HEALTH

5. PRIORITIZE FAMILY
AND FRIENDS

6. ENJOY THE
NEW SEASON

No one listens to unsolicited advice. Generally, people have to find the answers for themselves.

It felt like, in retrospect, I should have been more supportive in his choice of what to do. I think he would have benefitted from a little more downtime away from corporate life before jumping into something else. But things came together, and he was ready to ramp up.

I didn't have anybody to talk to who was in the same position as I was. The disconnect between my spouse being such an extrovert and me being such an introvert—I don't think most of our friends faced that much of a challenge. It was kind of a rude awakening for me that, "oh gosh, he's retired, and I don't really know what that means; are we moving or are we staying?" I wish I'd had someone to talk to just me, not both of us. I wish I'd had a book to read; I wish I'd had anything...other women who were going through it. I didn't have a group of women to just share what I was experiencing.

I should have stood up for myself and prepared for him to be at home. I should have thought about what that might mean. I don't think it would have been accurate, but it would have been easier to carve out more space for myself if I had thought about it ahead of time.

How well retirement goes depends on the relationship of the husband and wife, whether they've survived these many years with something intact. We are lucky, we have a great base to build on.

Retirement sounds so appealing; do what you want, when you want, or not. The reality is a different story. It's worth the struggle when there is one, but getting there is not always pretty. My advice? Think about retirement ahead of time! Force the discussion if you must. Get rid of pie-in-the-sky notions of wonderfulness. Be honest! Be practical. Get help if help is available. You're going need it.

1. PREPARE FOR A RANGE
OF EMOTIONS

2. RETAIN YOUR
IDENTITY

3. COMMUNICATE
AUTHENTICALLY

Before they retire, encourage them to develop outside interests, or any interests, even if its reading in their own home, or art, or whatever.

I wish we had recognized that we needed help instead of trying to reinvent the wheel. We were each frustrated because the other wasn't filling the role we wanted them to, or had expected them to. We thought it would be automatic, instead of communicating honestly and then compromising. Call in the professionals!

My hope would be that my husband would really be able to channel whatever he gained from working for more than three decades as he finds his new life. And only he can do that; I can't do that for him.

I think certainly there will be another season when we both have other things we want to pursue, but we haven't quite gotten to that phase yet.

You're going to have the incredibly wonderful time—just not in the same way. Try to seek out people who are going through transitions gracefully or who have done them. I found it helpful to seek out people who were newly retired.

Acceptance

The universal response we received from our spouse/partners was the constant of change. It seems to be true that one season evolves into the next and exploration, communication, and preparation were cited as key.

He enjoys being productive. I hear him tell his friends and family, I'm glad I have something to do. He has friends that are still working various careers, and he can see that a lot of them are a lot happier than the ones that are home not doing anything except recreational or whatever.

4. REKINDLE YOUR RELATIONSHIP
AND ATTEND TO YOUR HEALTH

5. PRIORITIZE FAMILY
AND FRIENDS

6. ENJOY THE
NEW SEASON

If you aren't happy with your employment years, you won't be happy in your retirement years. Choose to be happy, no matter what you are doing.

I would love it if he would initiate, "let's do such and such today or tomorrow." I always must do the initiating, and he goes along, and that's not going to change.

Love what you're doing, but don't hold on too tightly, because things do change, life does move on.

I admit I am a little disappointed (resentful?) that he reneged on his promise to spend retirement with me, but after two years of full-time togetherness, it didn't take long to see this was a gift to both of us! He was happy! And I didn't have to entertain him full time! Everybody wins.

I tired of waiting for the day he was going to retire. And then he retired!

They need to have their hobbies started before they retire. Every time people would ask him how it is going, he was just glowing because he wanted to get up and practically run to the garage every morning and start working on his hobbies. When I hear people talk about someone who's retired and they are kind of lost, I'm glad he didn't go through that. He's not had any of that "I'm lost time." I'm worried that I will, because I don't have a hobby.

Gratitude

Our study group was thankful for many things, but most-often cited appreciation for their retiring executive. When expressed fully, participants said they admired their partner and enjoyed sharing experiences throughout their relationships but in a new way, with a different cadence and presence of person. However, the single most important element of retirement was having the gift of time to invest in their relationship, self, family, and community.

We didn't feel like we were influencing people or touching their lives when he was working. But we had and still are.

I think his timing was perfect for his retirement. I think our relationship is even better and stronger than it ever was, and it was a very healthy happy relationship.

We have so enjoyed sharing life and doing things together. I am just grateful for it. Just really grateful.

He shared with me what his plan was, and I think I just, I bought it hook, line, and sinker. I had faith in him that he knew what he was doing and what he wanted to do. I even recognized, and I think this is somewhat important too, that sometimes spouses don't recognize the gift the spouse has—you know what I'm saying, you take it for granted.

Just because he stopped working, his gifts are still there. His gifts of leadership and building relationships and teams are an important part of who he is. This is the space where that's all going to be put to good work. I often tell him, who's to say the last 30 years weren't the build-up to the real work in your life—which is now.

Try to be mindful of what you're going through and be grateful, but know that things are going to change, and life moves on. Whatever your spouse or partner is doing, they're not going to do that forever.

He thought maybe he needed to work for a few more years. He had thought it would be more golf and occasional phone consultations or meetings with someone. Then things picked back up. I have watched from the sidelines how it's been good for him. He loves sharing his experiences and he's such a smart person. People recognize that. It wasn't anything he actively sought, it was more people finding him and asking him to do things.

We really count our blessings. Things can change so instantly in your life, and we're enjoying every day.

CHAPTER THREE

Additional Perspectives of Executive Spouses

When we created a list of those we would ask to participate in the study group, two people immediately came to mind: **Carol Braksick** and **Claire Peppercorn**. Both were married to executives who had transitioned, and both were well beyond the first next season and onto third and fourth seasons following the retirement of their spouse. The two responses shared below were so rich that we decided to include them in the exact form in which they were received.

Carol Braksick sent this essay prior to her interview for this book. After compiling the data from our study group, we felt her essay eloquently expresses thoughts and feelings found in the responses of all of our participants. She included a brief autobiography that, coupled with the essay, gives us all a clear picture of what it takes to transition well. Her honesty is relatable, and her humor makes the truths she shares palatable.

MyNextSeason—RETIREMENT ESSAY—FEBRUARY 2017

My husband's retirement does not bring back good memories. His retirement was combined with back surgery and a long recovery. Two strikes!

Before he retired, we were interviewed for an article about retiring for our local newspaper. We were essentially going to just "wing it." He infamously stated for the article that, since his career had dictated our life together up until then, it was MY turn to have a lot of say in the retirement years. I'm sure he meant it at the time :). When the article came out, we were portrayed as the couple who had the wrong approach, and they were right about that!

While he retired from his company, I was still running MY "company," which was the household and every other area of our lives except his work. He was now on my "turf" where I was the expert in charge. He didn't even know how to navigate much of our town. He had only driven back and forth to work, to the airport, and to church! We had each been very competent CEOs. Which area was I supposed to give over to him when it was easier to do it myself? Okay, grocery shopping. He went grocery shopping for me every day! One day, I came home from a solo event to find that he had rearranged the spices, formerly arranged alphabetically, but newly arranged by "heat." From then on, I had to decide which had more "heat," cinnamon or nutmeg, etc. Both funny and frustrating.

We loved each other deeply, but how to retire together enjoyably? We didn't have a clue! What to do with him?!? If only there had been a "retirement counselor" available, or a book! We were trying to navigate this new world through trial and error. It might have been easier if he had been an avid golfer. That would have eaten some chunks of time. There are only so many trips you can take and then there's the long stretch of time until the next one.

We built a house which he poured himself into for a while. He went the route of serving on non-profit boards, but it didn't quite satisfy his level of energy and desire to make a difference.

Finally, an opportunity came along that was tailor-made. He was serving on a non-profit board that was struggling in its infancy. The Executive Director left the organization and so they were looking for someone to take his place. My husband stepped into that void and served as its volunteer Executive Director for five years and continued to serve in other capacities after that. I admit to being a little disappointed (resentful?) that he reneged on his promise to spend retirement with me, but after two years of full-time togetherness, it didn't take long to see this was a gift for both of us! He was happy! And I didn't have to entertain him full time! Everybody wins. I'm sure I breathed a huge sigh of relief when he left for a real office every day. His new gig even required some travel on his part. We both had some space, literally and figuratively, now that we were no longer "joined at the hip." He even had a new assistant who jumped to do his bidding with "How high?" and "How soon?"

We learned a lot in the two years between career retirement and our next season. We learned it the hard way, though. Would we do it over any better? Not without help, we wouldn't. Even with empathy for each other, we didn't know how to get from "A" to "B." A sense of humor is essential but smiling through gritted teeth was also part of the mix.

I participated in his new activity when I cared to. It has been my choice. It has been a blessing to both of us because the results of his efforts still make an enormous difference around the world. He is retired from that organization, too, mostly because he is limited by a handicap. He is more content this time but is never idle.

We both feel good about what we've accomplished and what we can still contribute. When one person has a demanding career, it is easy to think the other person will wait until you have time to give to them. While I appreciated the fact that he was providing a very comfortable living for us, I did lead a separate but parallel life. We were novices when our lives needed to converge. Retirement sounds so appealing. Do what you want, when you want, or not. The reality is a different story. It is worth the struggle when there is one but getting there is not always pretty.

My advice? Think about retirement ahead of time! Force the discussion if you have to. Get rid of "pie in the sky" notions of wonderfulness. Be honest! Be practical. Get help if help is available. You're gonna need it.

BIO

Carol Braksick is a "retired housewife" who enjoyed parenting three wonderful children while her husband, Norm, pursued a career which culminated in a CEO capacity. Her greatest joy is spending time with their grandchildren and a number of volunteer activities. Their parallel lives resulted in a retirement which surprised them by their lack of preparedness for it. Loving each other deeply was not sufficient to traverse a new road smoothly. They had always heard "You can't live on love" and now they were experiencing it. A good sense of humor and doing their best to accommodate the other helped, but there was still a sense of frustration. The advice she gives and wishes she had when they needed it: Get help wherever you can find it!

....

John Peppercorn, who sent the email below, was a client of Leslie Braksick's when she was CEO of a firm she co-founded (CLG) prior to MyNextSeason. Leslie and her family relocated to the West Coast to support him and Chevron Chemical Company while he was CEO. Leslie's office was three doors down from John's and they worked closely together. There were some tender life events for the Braksick family during the three years she worked with John, and he and his wife Claire were incredibly kind and supportive.

In support of this research, Leslie sent an email to Claire so that we might do an interview with her. John then intercepted that email and sent a heartwarming response. We thought you would enjoy his humor, perspective, and admiration for his spouse as much as we did. (He ALWAYS sent in his emails using all caps!)

LESLIE,

IT'S GREAT TO HEAR FROM YOU AND KNOW THAT YOU AND THE FAMILY ARE WELL.

MY ACTIVITY NOW IS CHURCH RELATED AND I CONTINUE
ON THE EXECUTIVE COMMITTEE OF OUR BUSINESS SCHOOL.
I ALWAYS THOUGHT HARD WORK GENERATED INCOME BUT
AM FINDING THE OPPOSITE WITH BOTH THE CHURCH AND
BUSINESS SCHOOL. THESE GUYS, IN ADDITION TO EDUCATION
AND RELIGION, REALLY KNOW HOW TO GET INTO ONE'S
POCKET BOOK.

I'M PLEASED TO HEAR YOU ARE STARTING A NEW ENDEAVOR
BUT FROM MY PERSPECTIVE IT'S THE GUYS WHO NEED THE
HELP. I USED TO HAVE SOME AUTHORITY BUT TODAY IT'S
LIMITED AT BEST. I USED TO HAVE A SECRETARY BUT TODAY?????

I COULD CLOSE MY OFFICE DOOR FOR A LITTLE PEACE AND
QUITE BUT TODAY?????

I USED TO HAVE A LIST OF THINGS I NEEDED TO DO BUT
TODAY MY LIST IS MUCH LONGER AND FOR 2. I USED TO HAVE
MEETINGS AND TALK ABOUT BUSINESS RESULTS, PROJECTS,
AND PRODUCT MARGINS. TODAY WE HEAR ABOUT WHO
DIED AND WHAT MEDICINE DO YOU TAKE. I KNOW YOU ARE
SAD AND SORRY FOR ME AND WILL BE INSPIRED TO HAVE
A 2 FOR 1 OFFERING THAT INCLUDES ADVICE FOR MALE
RETIREES. IN THIS DAY AND AGE, I'M SURE YOU DONT WANT
TO DISCRIMINATE AGAINST ANYONE AND RUN THE RISK OF
RETIRED MALE EXECTUTIVES PROTESTING IN FRONT OF YOUR
BEAVER CREEK HOME. I CAN VISUALIZE PROTEST SIGNS THAT
READ---MADAM BRAKSICK, ORGANIZES SPOUSES OF RETIRED
EXECUTIVES---NO BREAKFAST OR LUNCH, YOU CAN'T PLAY
GOLF WITH THE LADIES AND DON'T SHOW FOR LUNCH, IF YOU
GAIN A LITTLE WEIGHT I'M NOT MOVING THE BUTTONS ON
YOUR PANTS, YOU KNOW WHERE THE CLEANERS IS LOCATED,
AND ON AND ON IT GOES.

ISN'T CHANGE DIFFICULT.

BY THE WAY MY RETIRMENT HAS GONE VERY WELL IN ALL
RESPECTS. CLAIRE HAS BEEN GREAT. I'M A LUCKY GUY WITH A
LOT OF COMPANY AND OTHER FRIENDS. THE ENTIRE FAMILY IS

CLOSE AND ENJOYS ONE ANOTHER. I THINK AT SOME POINT IN ALL THIS THE FAMILY IS FAR AND AWAY THE MOST IMPORTANT THING. IT'S THE GLUE THAT SUPERCEEDS ALL ELSE.

WOULD LOVE TO SEE YOU ALL AGAIN AND WISH YOU THE BEST IN THE NEW ENDEAVOR,

JOHN

P.S. ALL HUGS ARE READLY ACCEPTED.

CHAPTER FOUR

Through the Lens of Advisors

A t MyNextSeason, each retiring executive is partnered with a dedicated Advisor, a former corporate leader who has transitioned to his/her own next season. Their work together is anchored in our transition methodology, and the partnership formed gives every retiring executive the benefit of having a confidant as well as access to the body of experience of someone who has "been there and done that."

Our Advisors have gained a wealth of insight in working with retiring executives and their spouse/partners. As part of our retirement transition methodology, there may be the opportunity for the executive and the spouse/partner to participate in a session together with the Advisor. We use the PARTNER Model, detailed in Chapter 5, so that both partners can work through ideas and concerns in order to move forward with greater clarity and expectations. Advisors are well-equipped to sense potential issues and support early thoughts and ideas using this model and methodology.

We asked our Advisors, who have worked with hundreds of executives across industries and functional areas, to answer three questions meant to identify common areas of interest and concern. We noted themes in the Advisors' answers that suggest there are common reactions and concerns to be explored and discussed between you and your retiring executive. The questions we asked were:

1. What issues are most often discussed regarding spouse/partners, or between spouse/partners?

2. What are the issues not being discussed, but should be? (what is the elephant in the room that everyone is ignoring?)

3. Is there anything we can do to help these discussions with your clients?

Theirs is a powerful vantage point, and we are thankful that they shared their experiences with us. Their responses to our questions are detailed below and organized under the same six themes as our study group. We found it interesting how much their observations aligned with responses from our participants.

1. Prepare for a Range of Emotions

Questions and concerns reported by the spouse/partner as observed by the Advisor

- What will the executive do when there is no job to go to—both a time and space issue

- How the retiring executive will react in an environment where they are not in charge of everything

- Concern that the executive won't retire well because they are wired to work

- Concern that the retiring executive is flexible enough to adapt to life after a hard-charging career

- Reluctance to participate in retirement discussions with executive and Advisor, as corporate cultures have supported public displays of support only; thus, a spouse session with both an Advisor and executive is initially uncomfortable for the spouse/partner

Retiring executive's thoughts as observed by the Advisor

- Wresting with the compulsion to work versus the need to work

- This is overwhelming—how do we start to plan?

2. Retain Your Identity

Spouse/partner's thoughts as observed by the Advisor

- Desire to maintain individual activities while adding activities as a couple

- Need to create space both physically and emotionally for both to thrive

- How to integrate the executive into the community in which the spouse/partner is embedded—does the executive want to become involved, and what does that look like?

- Concern about routines being disrupted

3. Communicate Authentically

Spouse/partner's thoughts as observed by the Advisor

- Allocating and committing time to certain commitments and being accountable for spending the time as planned

- Unspoken and thus different expectations for life after retirement

- Ensuring their needs are included in discussions and plans

Thoughts observed by the Advisor from the executive

- Trusting the spouse/partner to be a continuing source of insight and information, including accurately assessing gifts and strengths

- Acknowledging that the spouse/partner's participation in creating a plan for the season after retirement will yield a better plan

- Expectation that the spouse/partner will be honest in their feedback

4. Rekindle Your Relationship and Attend to Your Health

Thoughts observed by the Advisor from the executive

- Concern that instead of one big job, the executive will have many little jobs, spending just as much time working in retirement

- Exploring how the retiring executive can support the spouse/partner in their next season goals

5. Prioritize Family and Friends

As observed by the Advisor relative to the thoughts shared by both executive and spouse/partner

- Time allocation—time for my interests and time for family and friends

6. Enjoy the New Season

As observed by the Advisor relative to the couple's thoughts

- Angst over the ability to adapt to a next season by both parties

  - Fear over loss of income with the retirement

  - Fear the executive will keep working and not be able to relax into a first next season

Advisors reported a pattern of a reluctance by some executive clients in involving their spouse/partner in retirement planning. Several reasons were cited for this reluctance:

- The executive's initial plans for retirement involved executive engagements such as consulting, board work, teaching, and speaking. Because the spouse/partner likely was not involved in their career development, the executive did not think to include them in what was, to the executive, an extension of their career.

- The retiring executive was anxious and unsure what they will choose to do next. Because these executives shape vision and lead people and processes with great success, they became anxious in the uncertainty of the transition. They wanted to figure out what their next season looked like and then share the vision with their spouse/partner.

Discussion concerning investments, spending, and lifestyle was reported by our Advisors as necessary to the planning process for both executive and spouse/partner. The Advisors cited knowledge of finances and estate planning, and sharing thinking about them, creates the dynamic needed for an easier transition for both parties. Finally, Advisors cited patience and trust as key to creating dialogue to clarify thoughts and facilitate planning so that the couple can move forward with shared expectations.

CHAPTER FIVE

Partner Model

We offer a Spouse Session as part of our support services for retiring executives and their spouse/partner. Advisors lead this session with the purpose of helping both executive and spouse/partner align on their thoughts and begin to put a plan together. Our Advisors use this model and find the structure leads to robust and fruitful discussions between couples.

PARTNERing During Transition

Spouse/partners have played vital roles throughout the lives and careers of most executives. In a study conducted in 2008, 27 sitting CEOs were asked, *Who do you rely on most as your trusted advisor?* Nearly all responded by saying their most trusted confidant was their spouse. They went on to say they could not have navigated their careers without the full partnership, counsel, and ever-present support of their spouse.

The less-talked-about storyline, however, is the myriad of other roles you've undertaken separate from being the spouse of an executive. Frequently, busy executives are unable to engage as much as they would like in the details of home and family life. Whether both people have been working or just one, the demands on each often necessitate a "divide and conquer" lifestyle.

The career transition of your spouse has a huge impact on him/her, but it also has a major impact on you and on your lives together. The clarity of purpose, rules of the journey, and destination are all reset with this transition. For some, new fears emerge about how decisions will be made, what life will look like post-transition, how both of you will adjust, and how you will find new rhythms.

The single action found to be most universally helpful is to talk about the transition. It is also useful to develop a plan and continually refine that plan. Identify the concerns. Identify the hopes and dreams. Discuss options. Be open when things are working or not working. Keeping the lines of communication wide open is critical to the successful transition of both you and your spouse.

Like many things in life, we have found it helpful to have a structure for conversation about the future to ensure that the dreams and concerns of both of you are considered in the planning phase. We offer the acronym PARTNER as a framework to guide your conversations and early planning efforts.

Priorities	What priorities and goals do we have for this next season?
Alternatives	What alternatives do we have in how we spend our time?
Realities	What current realities/constraints do we have to work within?
Togetherness	What things do we want to achieve together?
Non-togetherness	What things do we wish to pursue independently?
Events and actions	What are our actions/next steps?
Revisiting our plan	When will we revisit our plan to see how we are doing?

Working Through Your PARTNER Framework

Below is a framework to guide your conversation with your spouse/partner as you assemble a shared vision and plan for your next season. It is helpful to work through the framework independently first, and then discuss it together as you pull together a shared plan.

Priorities	What are your individual priorities for this next season? What are your priorities as a couple? Write your top-ten list, both individually and as a couple.
Alternatives	You have considered what you might do in this next phase of your life. What are your ideas? How will you spend your time? Where will you live? To what will you dedicate your time and resources?

Realities	What current realities/concerns do you have as you enter your next season?
	What realities must you navigate as you make your plans? Are there constraints you must work with, like aging parents or health concerns?
	Or that you want to work with, like proximity to children or not-forprofits you have committed to?
	Note: Do not rush through this phase. It is important to understand one another's concerns entering this phase—and to openly acknowledge variables that enable or constrain your options.
Togetherness	Some things you will want to do together, whereas other activities you will opt to pursue independently. What activities do you hope to share?
Non-togetherness	Likewise, what do you see yourselves doing independently?
	Note: Healthy independence is extremely important in this phase of life. You have each carved independent paths, and you need to honor those desires and commitments as well as adding new ones together.
Events	What actions or next steps do you need to take in light of what you've discussed/agreed to here?
Revisiting our plan	When will you revisit what you've discussed/agreed to here, to see if adjustments need to be made?

Your Unsung Hero

by Leslie W. Braksick, Ph.D.

In our thoughtful moments, we acknowledge that any victory requires the support of a village. Business (not to mention life!) is a team sport, and every successful leader has a dedicated supporting cast who helps them get there.

Within that amazing cast of supporters, there is one unsung hero who stands above all others in enabling an executive's success: the "spouse."

(Please note: I am the last person who would pen a sexist column! I use the term "spouse" and the pronoun "she" simply to spare you the annoyance of constantly seeing "she/he" or "spouse/partner." But rest assured: my words apply equally to all of you "he" spouse/partners out there. I know, because my husband is one!)

Profile of Your Unsung Hero

Your spouse must be as strong as an ox, with shoulders broad enough to carry your burdens as well as her own—and your children's. She must have the flexibility of Gumby, the hospitality know-how of Martha Stewart, and the smarts of a weekend news anchor. She is expected to be attractive, well-coiffed, and have the stamina of a marathon runner.

When among your team and board members, she is expected to adore each of them equally. Privately, you rely on her impeccable judgment to help shape your thinking about your team and board challenges.

Out of necessity, she is "single parent of the year," annually. She is the lone juggler of kids, house maintenance, and aging parents or extended family. You are always available on the other end of text messages, emails, or cell calls, but rarely do you have the bandwidth or flexibility to be the taxi service for doctor's appointments, gift buying/mailing, car repairs, soccer games, or teenage broken hearts.

She manages it all with grace and aplomb, on behalf of you both.

Celebrating Your Unsung Hero

Your spouse is unequivocally the unsung hero in your world. Her duty and service are immensely deserving of recognition and celebration—especially as you transition from your long-standing corporate career. She has been a tireless hero, without pay, title, or performance review. Thanks and gratitude to her are likely long overdue. So, what form of thanks is best?

First, there is no substitute for words of appreciation. Whether you choose to write a letter or find a card, or simply express your sentiments directly, there is no close second to a personalized, sincere, thoughtful expression of gratitude. Be specific. Detail your feelings with words and examples. Ensure that the intensity of your words mirrors the intensity of your appreciation.

Second, show your appreciation by planning something special that your spouse would love. The basic rule is this: "Reinforcers" (things that make one feel appreciated) are determined by the receiver (your spouse), not by the giver (you). So, while you personally may love a "his-and-her big game hunting expedition," she may prefer a weekend for two in NYC that includes a quiet dinner and a Broadway show.

So make it all about her. Do something that she would find special and memorable, and demonstrate your unwavering appreciation by giving her top priority. Toast her for all that she has sacrificed in support of your career success.

And finally, devote the time, conversation, and planning for your Next Season together. Ask about her goals as you contemplate your own. Pause to honor both of your careers as you sit together to plan what's next, leaving room for continued, healthy independence.

There should be no greater early transition priority than celebrating the unsung hero in your life.

About the Author

Dr. Leslie W. Braksick is the Co-founder and Senior Partner of MyNextSeason (www.mynextseason.com), a company whose purpose is to help executives transition from careers oriented around productivity to lives anchored in purpose. Dr. Braksick may be reached at (412) 802–9196 or at leslie.braksick@mynextseason.com.

CHAPTER SIX

....

Closing Comments

We are thankful to the twenty-six spouse/partners who shared, with candor and thoughtfulness, the information reported in this book. We set out to capture the voices of those who had supported a retiring executive and what they experienced so that you might be better-equipped when you undertake this transition. Retirement upends life as we know it, which creates opportunities to explore.

We've shared information from these interviews with corporations and professional groups, knowing that this data has never before been collected and presented in this way. One question we are frequently asked is, "What are the takeaways?" Because we chose to let these articulate spouse/partners speak for themselves, rather than analyze their responses, we had not planned to draw any conclusions. However, after pouring over the data, we've distilled the information to five recommendations, applicable to both people in the relationship:

- Communicate

  - Early and often throughout the process, including sharing calendars

- Set expectations

  - By discussing joint and individual activities and interests

- Cede control over issues not important to you

- Separate offices/workspaces

- Rekindle the relationship

There is no question that our study group moved through the retirement transition with humor, creativity, and flexibility, plus the occasional reset and realignment. With concern for the family, the executive, and for themselves, they each honored their needs and those of their partner in ways that were unique to their situation.

Allen and Carol Kelly, one married couple who have enjoyed living around the world and are full of curiosity, mirth, and insight, shared with us their unique and successful method to communicate, set expectations, and transition to a fruitful and active time of life. They used a trifold project board and sticky notes to discuss, over a glass of wine on Friday evenings, what they each wanted to do and accomplish when he retired: separate walking groups (one for him and one for her); getting healthy; a long-planned-for art gallery business; speaking engagements; home renovations; and travel. These were shared and placed on the project board in the appropriate spots: now, later, back burner, need more information, etc. (A video of Allen and Carol talking about their plans and their project board is on our website, mynextseason.com. You also can find articles on legacy, expectations in retirement, and other salient subjects on the website.)

Another executive we supported wanted to set up a routine check-in with his spouse and children to ensure he was meeting his own desire to renew the partnership and prioritize his children. He used the birthdays of his family members as a gentle reminder to keep himself accountable to his goals.

We hope that you can relate to some of the feelings and challenges our study group navigated along the way. We are thankful to them and appreciate the care and courage with which they answered our questions, including sharing the moments that were uncomfortable and, at times, painful. Our hope is that the collective experiences shared on these pages are helpful as you approach or move through your first season of retirement, so this season and the ones following are satisfying and fulfilling.

ABOUT MYNEXTSEASON

MyNextSeason recognizes the power of having an approach that is both disciplined and flexible to help clients successfully discern, design, and realize next season goals and roles. Clients are matched with a carefully chosen Advisor who will customize the MyNextSeason experience to best meet individual needs, situations, and desired pacing.

Retirement Transition Support

MyNextSeason helps leaders transition by offering varying levels of advising, networking support, state-of-the-art rebranding, opportunity research, and board search guidance. Our goal is for clients to realize whatever goals they set for their next phase of life.

Early Career

MyNextSeason's early career programs help young professionals and college students alike realize enhanced clarity, self-confidence, capabilities, and direction to gain a competitive advantage in their lives and careers.

Executive Advising

The later stages of an executive's career often require specific actions to benefit both the individual and the company. Whether it's carefully constructed coaching, moving to a new role, or attaining a board seat to allow continued growth while still in role, MyNextSeason has a cadre of seasoned executive advisors who stand ready to help.

If you have interest in learning more about MyNextSeason services, call **412.802.9196** or contact us at **info@mynextseason.com**.

ABOUT THE AUTHOR

As Director of External Engagement, Debbie Dellinger supports clients in identifying, preparing for, and connecting to a variety of purposeful and fulfilling opportunities. In addition to working 1:1 with hundreds of executives, she leads a team of transition specialists, researchers, and senior writers in offering not-for-profit and board strategy, networking practices, and rebranding materials that position cumulative career success to achieve new goals. Attentive and thorough, she consistently draws from more than thirty years of expertise leading and serving not-for-profit organizations and earlier corporate experience to meet each client where they are.

The creator of multiple innovative additions to MyNextSeason's suite of services, Debbie has been instrumental in the company's evolution. She established an executive-on-loan program with nationally renowned not-for-profit organizations and launched a variety of tools to support individual client needs including network mapping, value proposition development, and thought leadership. She has cultivated numerous strategic relationships with consulting firms, incubators, and philanthropic partners, and established a portfolio of relevant internships for both college students and young professionals. She is dedicated to matching the wealth of experience possessed by transitioning executives and young professionals with organizations where their abilities can make a meaningful and mutually beneficial impact.

Debbie brings a passion built on decades of not-for-profit service to her role at MyNextSeason. Previously, she served as the Lay Leader of Education and Life Skills at the nation's largest United Methodist Church, where she also managed a volunteer program that partnered with three school districts and continues to impact 2,200 children in the Kansas City Metro area. Still deeply involved in giving back, she serves on the Resurrection Foundation Board and is an advisor to the church's "Crossroads" retirement offering, applying MyNextSeason thinking to support retirees throughout the community.

In addition, Debbie spent five years as Board Chair of The Hope Center, a not-for-profit dedicated to developing healthy communities in Kansas City through outreach, where her priorities included a charter school, a health clinic, and economic development and housing initiatives. Before transitioning to her career serving not-for-profits, Debbie led a software development center for GE Consulting and supported federal benchmarks for Honeywell Information Systems.

Debbie is the author of "*A Lens into Executive Retirement from the Spouse/Partner Perspective*" and a contributing author to "*Living into Your Next Season: Moving Forward After the Crisis of 2020.*" She received a BA in creative writing, journalism, and psychology from Ohio Wesleyan University. She and her husband, Bob, have four adult children, Rob, Doug, Megan and Patrick.

ACKNOWLEDGMENTS

This book is in your hands today as the result of a group of knowledgeable and caring experts who believe the seasons following retirement can be rewarding, purposeful, engaging, and sometimes challenging for both the executive and those who care about him/her. These experts, colleagues, and friends of MyNextSeason, specialize in transitions and include our Advisors, Co-Founders, and the External Engagement team who rebrand and support our clients' exploration of the many possibilities following a high-octane career. Each plays an important role in ensuring our clients and their significant others have the resources to create a purposeful first season and the tools to ensure that the discernment and implementation process is repeatable and may be used for additional seasons to follow.

My sincere gratitude to the following people for their amazing support:

….**Rani Lange** for being a collaborative partner in External Engagement and transcribing all of the interviews accurately while maintaining her equanimity throughout even when she worked in the car on the way to family holidays.

….**Mary Jones**, MyNextSeason Intern and rising senior at the College of William & Mary for her organization and updates of the participant study groups' bio and pictures.

….**Jeannie Hodes** for organizing and shaping the material as well as seeing and confirming the natural patterns in the data so that the information could be organized cohesively.

….**Jean Brinkmann**, **Dick Downen**, **Mark Linsz**, **Mike Sharp**, and **Burnet Tucker** – all MyNextSeason Advisors who have supported many executives and given me insights into the needs and desires of their transitioning clients and the spouse/partners.

….**Valerie Johnson** who interviewed five participants for this book using the specific questions asked of our study group as part of her work for the MyNextSeason project *Reflections on the Journey from Executive Spouses*.

….**Amy Baldwin**, a master of process and creativity, who organized and quarterbacked the work of pulling this book together in its final form. You are the best.

….**Jim Scattaregia** for his beautiful work in creating a book out of digital files while attending to the many details that allow us a good read.

….**Mark Linsz**, Co-Founder and Senior Managing Partner of MyNextSeason for both his leadership and support of this project. His intellect and creativity are embedded in MyNextSeason's DNA and inspire me to ensure our clients receive the best of what we offer in transition support.

….**Leslie Braksick**, Co-Founder and Senior Partner of MyNextSeason for her rock-solid ability to envision what can be and then how it can be better. She brought perspective and practical wisdom to this project and reached out to colleagues and clients to share their experiences as participants in the study group. Her ability to see and understand the potential of people is a pillar on which all of our work at MyNextSeason is based. I am blessed to call her my friend.

….**Sharon Ingles** and **Kathryn Trice** whose skills, coordination, and attention-to-detail make everything at MyNextSeason efficient and enjoyable.

….Three boys and a girl, who make up **D Team**, for their support and encouragement. Because they believe, I do too.

…The participants for trusting me and sharing their experiences so that you, the reader, can be part of the transition with your spouse/partner to a purpose filled and fulfilling next season.

BY SAME AUTHOR
AND MYNEXTSEASON COLLEAGUES

The coronavirus pandemic is an "intervention" unlike any other of our generation. Where do we go from here? What will we, individually and collectively, carry forward? The authors of *Living Into Your Next Season* specialize in life and career transitions and have brought their voices together to support your personal reflection and transformation.

For more info visit:
livingintoyournextseason.com

Your Next Season is a groundbreaking guidebook for the single greatest transition in an executive's adult life: retirement. Includes advice and insights gathered from hundreds of interviews with executives who've transitioned from an all-consuming corporate career to a fulfilling and rewarding Next Season.

For more info on our transition support services, visit:
mynextseason.com

Both books are available on **Amazon.com**.